Until the Sun rises from the West

THE ISLAMIC PERSPECTIVE

KWAME NERO

author**HOUSE®**

AuthorHouse™
1663 Liberty Drive
Bloomington, IN 47403
www.authorhouse.com
Phone: 833-262-8899

Published by AuthorHouse 10/19/2020

ISBN: 978-1-6655-0338-9 (sc)
ISBN: 978-1-6655-0336-5 (hc)
ISBN: 978-1-6655-0337-2 (e)

Library of Congress Control Number: 2020919660

All Praise and Thanks is due to Allah. We seek His help and forgiveness, and we seek refuge in Allah from the evil within ourselves and the consequences of our evil deeds. Whoever Allah guides will never be led astray, and whoever Allah leads astray will never find guidance. I bear witness there is no God but Allah, alone without any partners, and I bear witness that Muhammad (peace and blessings be upon him) is His Servant and Messenger.

Allah Almighty said, "O you who Believe. Fear Allah as he has a right to be feared and do not die except as Muslims" (3:102)

And Allah Almighty said, "O people, fear your Lord, who created you from one soul and created from it its mate and dispersed from both of them many men and women. Fear Allah, through whom you ask one another and maintain family ties. Verily, Allah is ever watching over you." (4:1)

And Allah Almighty said, "O you who have faith, fear Allah and speak upright words. He will correct your deeds and forgive your sins. Whoever obeys Allah and His Messenger has won a tremendous victory." (33:70-71)

Verily, the most truthful speech is the Book of Allah, the best guidance is the guidance of Muhammad (peace and blessings be upon him), and the worst of affairs are newly invented matters. Every newly invented matter is a religious innovation, and every religious innovation is misguidance, and every misguidance is in the Hellfire.

To proceed,

Surah 6 Al-An'am, Ayat 158

هَلْ يَنْظُرُوْنَ اِلَّاۤ اَنْ تَأْتِيَهُمُ الْمَلٰٓئِكَةُ اَوْ يَأْتِيَ رَبُّكَ اَوْ يَأْتِيَ

بَعْضُ اٰيٰتِ رَبِّكَ ۙ يَوْمَ يَأْتِيْ بَعْضُ اٰيٰتِ رَبِّكَ لَا يَنْفَعُ نَفْسًا

اِيْمَانُهَا لَمْ تَكُنْ اٰمَنَتْ مِنْ قَبْلُ اَوْ كَسَبَتْ فِيْۤ اِيْمَانِهَا خَيْرًا ۗ قُلِ

﴾6:158﴿ انْتَظِرُوْۤا اِنَّا مُنْتَظِرُوْنَ

(6:158) What! Do they wait either for the angels to appear before them or for your Lord to come unto them or for some clear signs of your Lord to appear before them? When some clear signs of your Lord will appear, believing will be of no avail to anyone who did not believe before, or who earned no good deeds through his faith. Say: 'Wait on; we too are waiting.'

Surah 47 Muhammad 18

فَهَلْ يَنْظُرُونَ إِلَّا ٱلسَّاعَةَ أَن تَأْتِيَهُم بَغْتَةً فَقَدْ جَاءَ

أَشْرَاطُهَا فَأَنَّىٰ لَهُمْ إِذَا جَاءَتْهُمْ ذِكْرَىٰهُمْ

(47:18) Then do they await except that the Hour should come upon them unexpectedly? But already there have come [some of] its indications. Then what good to them, when it has come, will be their remembrance?

Abu Huraira reported: The Messenger of Allah, peace and blessings be upon him, said, "The Hour will not be established until the sun rises from the west. Thus, when it rises from the west all people together will believe, but on that day no soul will benefit from his faith if he did not believe earlier or earn good from his faith." (6:158)

Source: Sahih Muslim 157

Matthew 24:29 Immediately after the tribulation of those days shall the sun be darkened, and the moon shall not give her light, and the stars shall fall from heaven, and the powers of the heavens shall be shaken:

30 And then shall appear the sign of the Son of man in heaven: and then shall all the tribes of the earth mourn, and they shall see the Son of man coming in the clouds of heaven with power and great glory.

31 And he shall send his angels with a great sound of a trumpet, and they shall gather together his elect from the four winds, from one end of heaven to the other.

32 Now learn a parable of the fig tree; When his branch is yet tender, and putteth forth leaves, ye know that summer is nigh:

33 So likewise ye, when ye shall see all these things, know that it is near, even at the doors.

34 Verily I say unto you, This generation shall not pass, till all these things be fulfilled.

35 Heaven and earth shall pass away, but my words shall not pass away.

36 But of that day and hour knoweth no man, no, not the angels of heaven, but my Father only.

Umar ibn al-Khattab reported: We were sitting with the Messenger of Allah, peace and blessings be upon him, one day when a man appeared with very white clothes and very black hair. There were no signs of travel on him and we did not recognize him. He sat down in front of the Prophet and rested his knees by his knees and placed his hands on his thighs. The man said, "O Muhammad, tell me about Islam." The Prophet said, "Islam is to testify there is no God but Allah and Muhammad is the Messenger of Allah, to establish prayer, to give charity, to fast the month of Ramadan, and to perform pilgrimage to the House if a way is possible." The man said, "You have spoken truthfully." We were surprised that he asked him and said he was truthful. He said, "Tell me about faith." The Prophet said, "Faith is to believe in Allah, his angels, his books, his messengers, the Last Day, and to believe in providence, its good and its evil." The man said, "You have spoken truthfully. Tell me about excellence." The Prophet said, "Excellence is to worship Allah as if you see him, for if you do not see him, he surely sees you." The man said, "Tell me about the final hour." The Prophet said, "The one asked does not know more than the one asking." The man said, "Tell me about its signs." The Prophet said, "The slave girl will give birth to her mistress and Master, that you will see barefoot, naked, and dependent shepherds compete in the construction of tall buildings." Then, the man returned and I remained. The Prophet said to me, "O Umar, do you know who he was?" I said, "Allah and his messenger know best." The Prophet said, "Verily, he was Gabriel who came to teach you your religion."

Source: ṢAḥīḥ Muslim 8
Grade: Sahih (authentic) according to Muslim

Introduction

Islam (total submission to Allah) is one of the abrahamic faiths from the line of Ishmeal (AS) and all of its practices somehow go back to Abraham (AS), his wife Hagar, and Ishmael (AS). Islam is based on five basic principles

1. Monotheistic worship/ singling out God from all other creation (the Shahada -there is no deity worthy of worship except God and Muhammad is his last and final messenger)

2. The Prayer (Salaat is observed five times a day) by all Muslims at specific times according to the Sun and the Moon and it's done in a very specific manner, adhering to all of the prerequisites (you must wash before every prayer), and very specific modes of transport (one of the only ancient religions which still holds on to the practice of bowing one's face before the Lord).

3. Poor Dues (Zakaat) is obligatory on every Muslim who is pubescent which is simply 2.5% of the surplus of wealth and is normally given to the religious leader which is dispersed amongst the community to only 8 categories of individuals. The Quran says in chapter Al-Tawbah, 9:60 **"Indeed, [prescribed] charitable offerings are only [to be given] to the poor and the indigent, and to those who work on [administering] it, and to those whose hearts are to be reconciled, and to [free] those in bondage, and to the debt-ridden, and for the cause of God,**

and to the wayfarer. [This is] an obligation from God. And God is all-knowing, all- wise.

4. Fasting (Saum) during the month of Ramadan to celebrate the first revelation of the Quran. It is said that the angel Gabriel went to Prophet Muhammad in the cave of Lights in the month of Ramadan and gave him the first words of inspiration from God. It's stated in a Hadith (book of narration) "The angel came to him and asked him to read. The Prophet replied 'I do not know how to read'. The Prophet added, 'The angel caught me (forcibly) and pressed me so hard that I could not bear it any more. He then released me and again asked me to read and I replied, "I do not know how to read". Thereupon he caught me again and pressed me a second time till I could not bear it any more. He then released me and again asked me to read, but again I replied, "I do not know how to read" (or what shall I read?). Thereupon he caught me for the third time and pressed me, and then released me and said: "Read, in the name of Your Lord, who created, created man from a clot. Read! And Your Lord is the most bountiful" ... (Bukhari). These verses are found in the Quran in chapter 96:1-5 **"Recite in the name of your Lord who created – Created man from a clinging substance. Recite and your Lord is the most Generous –Who taught by the pen – Taught man that which he knew not."**

Even though Prophet Muhammad had many miracles but he says that the Quran is the greatest miracle which had ever been given to any of the prophets. In the time of Moses the people had mastered the art of black magic and God gave Moses five specific miracles which defeated all the magic that was prevalent at this time. During the time of Jesus the people had mastered the art of Medicine but God gave Jesus the miraculous ability to heal the one with leprosy, bring sight to those born blind, raise the Dead and these Miracles surpassed all of the Medicine from that time all the way up till today, with all of our technology. During the time of prophet Muhammad the people had mastered the art of poetry and God sent the Quran which is miraculous in nature. It speaks about science that to this day scientists are just coming to realize. It confirms what came before it meaning the Old Testament and New Testament. It is said that God assigned it to be delivered from an angel Gabriel to a man (Prophet Muhammad), who could not read or write yet to this day the perfection has been unmatched by any author. Many Muslims memorize the whole Quran with all 114 chapters which is also miraculous in nature but even those who don't memorize the whole book must memorize portions of it to be used in their five daily prayers. The verses and chapters were delivered in a scattered arrangement according to events that happened in the life of prophet Muhammad since his prophethood of only 23 years. It is said that the Angel Gabriel would come and correct the Quran recitation with Prophet Muhammad every year in the month of Ramadan.

The staff of Moses is now gone from our presence and those who were brought back to life by Jesus have now passed on, all of these Miracles are preserved in the words of God known to Muslims as the Quran, the Everlasting miracle which will remain until the end of time.

5. The pilgrimage (Hajj) is obligatory on all Muslims who can afford to go to the Holy Land of Mecca and observe the rituals given to us by the family of Abraham. It is said that Abraham and his son Ishmael built the first house of God known to Muslims as the Kaaba. A stone or meteorite fell from the sky which they used to build his house with and God told him to call the people to his sacred house and since that calling people have visited

the Kaaba for pilgrimage. In the past pagan idolaters put their Idols there and worship in that location as well however Prophet Muhammad came and destroyed all the idols and made Mecca reserved for Muslims only and the worship of God Alone. These five categories comprised of the five pillars of Islam which is the meaning of Islam and is the aspects of the limbs. Meaning these are things that we must do. In addition there is the six articles of faith which every Muslim must believe in which are

1. Belief in Allah, The Only God
2. Belief in the Angels
3. Belief in Holy Books
4. Belief in the Prophets
5. Belief in the Day of Judgment
6. Belief in God's predestination

As it states in the narration (Hadith) Iman (faith) is that you believe in God and His Angels and His Books and His Messengers and the Hereafter and the good and evil fate [ordained by your God]. Many people don't believe that Muslims believe in the Bible or in Jesus but as you see it is in our fabric to believe in them and any Muslim who does not is not a true Muslim.

Shahada

<u>The fruit of Islam</u>

Allah said in Surah 24 ayats 24. **See you not how Allah sets forth a parable? A goodly word as a goodly tree, whose roots are firmly fixed, and its branches (reach) to the sky (i.e Very high). 25. Giving its fruit at all times, by the Leave of its Lord and Allah sets forth parables for mankind in order that they may remember.**

Ali bin Abi Talhah reported that Abdullah bin Abbas commented that Allah's statement, "a parable: a goodly word" refers to testifying to La ilaha illallah (none has the right to be worshipped but Allah) while," as a goody tree", refers to the believer, and that "whose roots is firmly fixed ", indicates that La ilaha illallah (none has the right to be worshipped but Allah) is firm in the believers heart, and "it's branches (reach) to the sky" means with which the believers work are ascended to heaven. The believer is just like the beneficial Date Tree, always having good actions ascending at all times, by day and by night.

Al-Bukhari recorded that Abdullah Bin Umar said, "we were with the Messenger of Allah (may peace and blessing be upon him) when he asked, Tell me about a tree that resemble the Muslim, the leave of which do not fall in the summer or winter and gives its fruit at all times by the leave of it's Lord."

Ibn Umar said, "I thought of the Date Palm tree, but felt shy to

1

answer when I saw that Abu Bakr and Umar did not talk". When they did not give an answer, the Messenger of Allah (may peace and blessing be upon him) said, "It is the Date Palm Tree". When we departed, I said to Umar, my father,' by Allah! I thought that it was the Date tree". He said, 'why did you not speak then?' I said, "I saw you were silent and I felt shy to say anything". Umar said 'Had you said it, it would have been more precious to me then such things (i.e. would have been very precious to me)'.

This La ilaha illallah is one of the first
words we hear when we are born:

Abu Rafi said: I saw the Apostle of Allah (may peace and blessing be upon him) Uttering the Call to prayer in the ear of Al-Hasan Bin Ali when Fatimah gave birth to him

Sunnah Abu Dawud
Vol.III p.1415 #5086

The Kalima of Tawheed la ilaha illallah is in the Called to prayer and Allah Taught us how to interact with our children through one of the slaves of Allah Luqman The Wise.

Allah said in Surah 31 Luqman 12. **And indeed we bestowed upon Luqman Al Hikmah (wisdom and religious understanding) saying: Give thanks to Allah. And whoever gives thanks, he gives thanks for the good of his own self. And whoever is unthankful, verily Allah is All-Rich (free of all needs) worthy of all praise.13. And remember when Luqman said to his son when he was advising him: "O my Son! Join not in worship others with Allah. Verily, joining others in worship with Allah is a great Zulm (wrong) indeed.**

It is narrated on the authority of Abu Huraira that the Messenger of Allah (may peace and blessing be upon him) Said: Faith is about seventy branches or is over sixty branches. The best of it is the saying that "there is no God but Allah" (La ilaha illallah). The humblest of which is the removal of what is injurious from the path and modesty is a branch of faith.

Sahih Muslim
Vol 1, p.58, #35R1

Narrated Ibn Umar(ra): Allah's Messenger (may peace and blessing be upon him) said: Islam is based on the following five (Pillars) principles:1. To testify that La ilaha illallah wa anna Muhammad-ar Rasul Allah (none has the right to be worshipped but Allah and that Muhammad is the Messenger of Allah). 2. Iqamat-as-Salat [to perform the compulsory congregational) Salaat (prayer)]. 3. To pay Zakat. 4. To perform Hajj (i.e. pilgrimage to Mecca). 5 To observe Saum (fasts according to Islamic teachings) during the month of Ramadan.

Sahih Al Bukhari
Vol.1 p.58, #8

Allah said in Surah 4 An Nisa 152. **And those who believe in Allah and his Messengers and make no distinction between any of them (Messengers). We shall give them their rewards; and Allah is Ever Oft-Forgiving, Most merciful (Ag Gafoorun Raheeman).**

Every Prophet was sent with La ilaha illallah.

Allah said in Surah 7 Al A'raf 73 **And to Thamud people, we sent their brother Salih. He said: O my people! Worship Allah! You have no other ilah (God) but him (La ilaha illallah: none has the right to be worshipped but Allah). Indeed there has come to you a clear sign (the miracle of the coming out of a huge she-Camel from the midst of a rock) from your Lord. This She-Camel of Allah is a sign unto** you; so you leave her to graze in Allah's earth, and touch her not with harm, lest a painful torment should seize you.

Allah said in Surah 3 Al-Imran 83. **Do they seek other than the religion of Allah (the true Islamic Monotheism -worshipping none but Allah alone), while to him submitted all creatures in the heavens and the earth, willingly or unwillingly. And to him shall they all be returned. 84. Say [O Muhammad (may peace and blessing be upon him)]:We believe in Allah and in what has been sent down to us, and what was sent down to Ibrahim (Abraham), Ishma'il (Ishmeal), Ishaq (Isaac), Ya'qub (Jacob) and Al-Asbat[the offspring of the twelve sons of Ya'qub (Jacob)] and what was given to Musa (Moses), Isa (Jesus) and the Prophets from their Lord. We make no distinction between one another among them and to Him (Allah) we have submitted in Islam. 85. And whoever seeks a religion other than Islam, it will never be accepted of him and in the hereafter he will be one of the losers.**

Jabir bin Abdullah narrated that the Messenger of Allah (may peace and blessing be upon him) said: Moses (as) said:O Lord! Teach me something that I can remember you with and I can supplicate you with. Allah said: "Say La ilaha illallah, O Musa". He (Musa) said: 'all of your servants say this'. He (Allah) said: If all of the dwellers of the seven heavens and those who dwell in there other than me and the seven Earths are put into one pan of the scale and La ilaha illallah is put into the other; La ilaha illallah would be heavier.

Ibn Hibbaan and Haakim.

Allah said in Surah 7 Al A'raf 59. **Indeed we sent Nuh (Noah) to his people and he said: "O my people! Worship Allah! You have no other ilah (God) but him (la ilaha illallah: none has the right to be worshipped but Allah). Certainly, I fear for you the torment of a Great Day!"**

4

Allah said in Surah 7 Al A'raf 65. **And to the Ad people we sent their brother Hud. He said: "O my people! Worship Allah! You have no other ilaha (God) but Him. La ilaha illallah (none has the right to be worship but Allah) Will you not fear Allah?**

Narrated Ibn Abbas (RA): When the Prophet (may peace and blessing be upon him) sent Mu'adh to Yemen, he said to him, "you are going to a nation from the people of the scripture, so let the first thing to which you will invite them is to testify the Tauhid Allah{i.e. La ilaha illallah(none has the right to be worshipped but Allah)]. If they acceptthat, tell them the Allah has enjoined on them five compulsory congregational Salaat (prayers) to be offered in one day and one night (24 hours). And if they offer their Salaat (prayer), tell them that Allah has enjoined on them Zakaat of their properties; and it is to be taken from the rich among them and given to the poor among them. And if they agree to that, then take from them Zakaat, but avoid the best property of the people.

Sahih Al-Bukhari
Vol. 9 p. 97, #7372

The benefit of Dying upon La ilaha illallah is great.

Mu'adh b. Jabal (ra) reported the Apostle of Allah (may peace and blessing be upon him) as saying: If anyone's last words are "There is no God but Allah", he will enter paradise.

Sunan Abu Dawud
Vol II p.887, #3110

La ilaha illallah has great benefit on the Day of Resurrection.

Abdullah ibn Amr ibn al-Aas (ra) said Allah's Messenger (may peace and blessing be upon him) said: A man from my nation will be called out in front of the whole of the creation on the Day of Resurrection. So ninety-nine scrolls will be laid out for him. Each of the scrolls will be as far as the eye can see. Then it will be said, "Do you deny anything from this?" So he will say, No, O my Lord". So it will be said, "Do you have any excuse or any good deed?" So it will be said: Yes indeed, you have good Deeds with us. You will not be wronged with regard to them". So a parchment will be brought out for him containing. I bear witness none has the right to be worshipped except Allah and I bear witness that Muhammad is his slave and his Messenger. So he will say, "O my Lord, what is this parchment in comparison to those scrolls"? So it will be said, "you will not be wronged". So the scrolls will be placed on one scale and that parchment will be placed on one scale. So the scrolls will be lighter and the parchment will outweigh".

> Narrated by Ahmad 6699 and At-Tirimidhi 2639
> Classed as saheeh by Shaykh Al-Albaani
> (may Allah have mercy on him)

It is our job to spread La ilaha illallah to our family, neighbour, and all that we encounter

Allah said in Surah 4 An Nisa 36. **Worship Allah and join none with Him in worship; and do good to parents, kinfolk, orphans, Al-Masakin (the poor), the neighbor who in near of kin, the neighbour who is a stranger, the companion by your side, the wayfarer (you meet), and those (slaves) whom your right hand possesses. Verily, Allah does not like such as are proud and boastful.**

Narrated Aishah (RA): The Prophet (may peace and blessing be upon him) said, "Jibriel (Gabriel) continued to recommend me about treating the neighbours kindly and politely, so much so that I thought he would order me to make them as my heirs".

Sahih Al-Bukhari

Vol. 8 p. 78, #6014

It is narrated on the authority of Anas b. Malik that the Prophet (may peace and blessing be upon him) observed: No one amongst you believes (truly) till one likes for his brother or for his neighbour what he loves for himself.

Sahih Muslim

Vol.I p.62, #45

It is narrated on the authority of Abu Huraira that the messenger of Allah (may peace and blessing be upon him) observed: He will not enter Paradise whose neighbor is not secure from his wrongful conduct.

Sahih Muslim

Vol. 1 p. 63, # 46

With so much differences of opinion in Islam many sects have become manifest, each one boosting in what they have. Each one claiming to be better than the other group but all Muslims confirm in their Shahaada that there is no God (ilah) /No diety worthy of worship except Allah and Muhammad (SAW) is his Slave/ servant/ and final Messenger of Allah so all the rights are due.

Narrated Maimun bin Siyah that he asked Anas bin Malik, "O Abu Hamza! What makes the life and property of a person sacred" he replied, "whoever says: La ilaha illallah (none has the right to be worshipped but Allah), faces our Qiblah (Ka'bah at Makkah) during the prayers, offers prayers like us and eats our slaughtered animals, then he is a Muslim, and has got the same rights and obligations as other Muslims have.

Sahih Al- Bukhari

Vol I p. 260, #393

Hazrat Usamah Ibn Zaid (RA) relates: Once the Holy Prophet (may peace and blessing be upon him) sent us on an expedition against the tribe of Juhainah living in the oasis of Huraqah. We reached their (water) springs in the morning. Ansar and I caught hold of one of their men, and when we had overpowered him, he recited La ilaha illallah [(The Kalima) There is none save Allah]. On hearing this the Ansari held back but I killed him with a stroke of my spear. On our return to medina, this incident was brought to the knowledge of the Holy Prophet (may peace and blessing be upon him). He asked me:'

O Usamah, did you kill him even after he had said La ilaha illallah (There is no god save Allah): I said: Messenger of Allah (may peace and blessing be upon him) he made the declaration only to save his life'. He said again: Did you kill him after he had affirmed: There is no God save Allah?' He sent on repeating this sentence till I felt that it would have been lesser if I had not accepted Islam before that day.

Bukhari & Muslim

Riyadh -us-Saleheen

Vol.I p. 236, #393

Tauhid

Tauhid (Oneness of God) is the essence of Life and La ilaha illallah (No god but God) is the only reason that Allah does not bring the sky crashing down. There isn't a hand span in the heavens except there is an Angel magnifying the worship of Allah. Every Prophet called their people to La ilaha illaallah and we the ummah (community) of Rasulullah (may peace and blessing be upon him) consider ourselves the inheritors of the

Prophets mission. So in that we too must call humanity to the oneness of Allah. Allah sent every Prophet with Tauhid and Allah will question their community whether they convey the Message.

Allah said in Surah 21 Al Anbiya 25. **And We did not send any Messenger before you {O Muhammad (may peace and blessing be upon him)} but we revealed to him (saying):" La ilaha illa Ana [none has the right to be worshipped but (Allah)], so worship me (Alone and none else)."**

And the only purpose mankind was created was to worship Allah

Allah said in Surah 51 Adh-Dharyat 56. **And I (Allah) created not the Jinn and mankind except that they should worship Me (Alone).**

The Prophets will be asked if they conveyed Tauhid

Noah was questioned

Narrated that Abu Sa'eed al-Khudri (RA) said: The Messenger of Allah (may peace and blessing be upon him) said: Nooh {Noah(AS)} will be called on the Day of Resurrection and it will be said to him: Did you convey (the Message)? He will say: 'Yes'. Then his people will be called and it will be said to them: 'Did he convey (the message) to you? They will Say: 'No warner came to us and no one came to us.". It will be said to Nooh {Noah(AS)}: Who will bear witness for you? He will say: Muhammad (may peace and blessing be upon him)and his Ummah'. He said: 'That is the words of Allah, "Thus we have made you a Just (the best) nation".

Al Bukhari 4487

Jesus called to Tauhid

Allah said in Surah 5 Al- Ma'idah 116. **And [beware the Day] when Allah will say, "O Jesus(AS), Son of Mary, did you say to the people, 'Take me and my mother as deities besides Allah?'" He will say, "Exalted are You! It was not for me to say that to which I have no right. If I had said it, You would have known it. You know what is within myself, and I do not know what is within Yourself. Indeed, it is You who is Knower of the unseen. 117. I said not to them except what You commanded me - to worship Allah, my Lord and your Lord. And I was a witness over them as long as I was among them; but when You took me up, You were the Observer over them, and You are, over all things, Witness.**

The Messenger of Allah spread Tauhid

All those who listen to me shall pass on my words to others and those to others again; and may the last ones understand my words better than those who listen to me directly. Be my witness, O Allah, that I have conveyed your message to your people". O People, no Prophet or Apostle will come after me and no new faith will be born. Reason well, therefore, O People, and understand words which I convey to you. I leave behind me two things, the Qur'an and my example, the SUNNAH and if you follow these you will never go astray.

(Reference: See Al-Bukhari, Hadith 1623, 1626, 6361) Sahih of Imam Muslim also refers to this sermon in Hadith number 98. Imam al-Tirmidhi has mentioned this sermon in Hadith nos. 1628, 2046, 2085. Imam Ahmed bin Hanbal has given us the longest and perhaps the most complete version of this sermon in his Masnud, Hadith no. 19774.)

Allah is out of the realm of Human perception

Narrated Abu Hurairah (RA) One day while the Prophet (may peace and blessing be upon him) was sitting out for the people, (a Man- the Angel) Jibril {Gabriel (AS)} came to him and asked, "What is faith? Allah's Messenger (may peace and blessing be upon him) replied, "Faith is to believe in Allah, His Angels, the meeting with Him, His Messenger, and to believe in Resurrection. Then he further asked, "what is Islam"? Allah's Messenger (may peace and blessing be upon him) replied, "To worship Allah (JalliJallun) Alone and none else, to perform the Salat (prayer) (Iqamat-as-Salat), to pay the Zakat and to observe Saum [fasts (according to Islamic teachings)] during the month of Ramadan." Then he further asked, what is Ihsan (Perfection)?" Allah's Messenger (may peace and blessing be upon him) replied, "To worship Allah (JalliJallun) as if you see him, and if you cannot achieve this state of devotion then you must consider that He is looking at you".

Sahih Al Bukhari
Book 1 p. 81, #50

So Alhumdulilllah we do have a Prophet who asked to see Allah in Surah 7 Al-A'raf 143. **And when Musa (Moses) came at the time and place appointed by Us, and his Lord (Allah) spoke to him; he said: "O my Lord! Show me (Yourself), that I may look upon You." Allah said: "You cannot see Me, but look upon the mountain if it stands still in its place then you shall see Me." So when his Lord appeared to the mountain, He made it collapse to dust; and Musa (Moses) fell unconscious. Then when he recovered his senses he said: "Glory is to you, I turn to you in repentance and I am the first of the believers."**

The appearance of Allah (JalliJallun) to the mountain was very little of Him. It was approximately equal to the tip of one's little finger as explained by the Prophet (may peace be upon him) when he recited the Verse in Tirmidhi.

11

There is also some ikteelaf (Difference of opinion) on whether The Messenger of Allah (may peace be upon him) saw Allah on Isra wa Miraj

It was narrated that Aa'ishah (RA) said "whoever told you that Muhammad (may peace be upon him) saw his Lord was lying. He said that no vision can grasp him in Surah 6 Al-An'am 102. **Such is Allah, your Lord! La ilaha illa Huwa (none has the right to be worshipped but He). The Creator of all things. So worship Him (Alone), and He is Wakil (Trustee, Disposer of affairs or Guardian) over all things. 103. No vision can grasp Him, but He grasps all vision. He is Al-Latif (the Most Subtle and Courteous). Well- Acquainted with all things.**

It was narrated that Abu Dharr (RA) said:" I asked the Messenger of Allah (may peace be upon him), " Did you see your lord? He said, ``He is veiled by Light, how could I see him."

Narrated by Muslim

Knowing that we can't see Allah discredits Uzair as a God for the Jews, Jesus (AS) as a God or the son of God to the Christians, the Dajjal (the antichrist) as a God as he will claim to all of humanity, and anyone else to be worshipped as a God. No deity is worthy of worship except Allah. This leads us to the need for Rules and Regulations on how we approach the worship of Allah. If we look at these nations who came before us we notice the Jews and Christian didn't follow Rules and Regulations.

Allah said in Surah 9 At-Taubah 30. **And the Jews say: 'Uzair (Ezra) is the son of Allah, and the Christians say: Messiah is the son of Allah. That is their saying with their mouths, resembling the saying of those who disbelieved aforetime. Allah's Curse be on them, how they are deluded away from the truth! 31. They (Jews and Christians) took their rabbis and their monks to be their lords** besides Allah (by obeying them in things which they made lawful or unlawful according to their own desires without being ordered by Allah), and (they also took as their Lord) Messiah, son of Maryam (Mary), while they (Jews and Christians) were commanded [in the Taurat (Torah) and the Injeel (Gospel)] to worship none but One Ilah (God- Allah) La ilaha illa Huwa (none has the right to be worshipped but He. Praise and glory is to Him (far above is He) from having the partners they associate (with him)."

It is extremely important to recreate the time when Allah sends these prophets to their people and take notice of the information they were assigned to relay. This information is revelation and instructions on how to approach this thing called life, by the creator of Life and Death. These Prophets are windows to get to know what Allah wants from us and binoculars on how to worship him correctly. As time progresses we lose sight of the truth that these prophets came with, but the blessing is that it (The Truth) was documented.

Anas reported that after the death of Allah's Messenger Abu Bakr said to 'Umar: Let us visit Umm Aiman as Allah's Messenger used to visit her. As we came to her, she wept. They (Abu Bakr and Umar) said to her: What makes you weep? What is in store (in the next world) for Allah's-Messenger is better than (this worldly life). She said: I weep not because I am ignorant of the fact that what is in store for Allah's Messenger (in the next world) is better than (this world), but I weep because the revelation which came from Heaven has ceased to come. This moved both of them to tears and they began to weep along with her.

Sahih Muslim 2454

As Jesus (AS) brought the revelation to the people they didn't think he was God or the son of God while he was on the Earth, even though today many do.

Mark 8:27-30 King James Version (KJV)

27 And Jesus went out, and his disciples, into the towns of Caesarea Philippi: and by the way he asked his disciples, saying unto them, Whom do men say that I am? 28 And they answered, John the Baptist; but some say, Elias; and others, One of the prophets. 29 And he saith unto them, But whom say ye that I am? And Peter answereth and saith unto him, Thou art the Christ. 30 And he charged them that they should tell no man of him.

The followers of Jesus Today and not on the same Path of the Followers of his time. Jesus (AS) told us that they will worship him in vain following the teaching of men and totally discrediting his actually teachings to worship God.

Matthew 15:1-20 King James Version (KJV)

15 Then came to Jesus scribes and Pharisees, which were of Jerusalem, saying, 2 Why do thy disciples transgress the tradition of the elders? for they wash not their hands when they eat bread. 3 But he answered and said unto them, Why do ye also transgress the commandment of God by your tradition? 4 For God commanded, saying, Honour thy father and mother: and, He that curseth father or mother, let him die the death. 5 But ye say, Whosoever shall say to his father or his mother, It is a gift, by whatsoever thou mightest be profited by me; 6 And honour not his father or his mother, he shall be free. Thus have ye made the commandment of God of none effect by your tradition. 7 Ye hypocrites, well did Esaias prophesy of you, saying, 8 This people draweth nigh unto me with their mouth, and honoureth me with their lips; but their heart is far from me. 9 But in vain they do worship me, teaching for doctrines the commandments of men. 10 And he called the multitude, and said unto them, Hear, and understand: 11 Not that which goeth into the mouth defileth a man; but that which cometh out of the mouth, this defileth

a man. 12 Then came his disciples, and said unto him, Knowest thou that the Pharisees were offended, after they heard this saying? 13 But he answered and said, Every plant, which my heavenly Father hath not planted, shall be rooted up. 14 Let them alone: they be blind leaders of the blind. And if the blind lead the blind, both shall fall into the ditch. 15 Then answered Peter and said unto him, Declare unto us this parable. 16 And Jesus said, Are ye also yet without understanding? 17 Do not ye yet understand, that whatsoever entereth in at the mouth goeth into the belly, and is cast out into the draught? 18 But those things which proceed out of the mouth come forth from the heart; and they defile the man. 19 For out of the heart proceed evil thoughts, murders, adulteries, fornications, thefts, false witness, blasphemies: 20 These are the things which defile a man: but to eat with unwashed hands defileth not a man.

They say Jesus Spoke in the cradle as a baby but they never ask what did he say;

> Allah tells us in Surah 19 Maryam **30 [Jesus] said,** "**Indeed, I am the servant of Allah. He has given me the Scripture and made me a prophet. 31 And He has made me blessed wherever I am and has enjoined upon me prayer and zakah as long as I remain alive 32 And [made me] dutiful to my mother, and He has not made me a wretched tyrant. 33 And peace is on me the day I was born and the day I will die and the day I am raised alive." 34 That is Jesus, the son of Mary - the word of truth about which they are in dispute. 35 It is not [befitting] for Allah to take a son; exalted is He! When He decrees an affair, He only says to it, "Be," and it is.**

His first words as a child is that he is the servant of Allah, as we all should be! The Meccan Pagans also fail to follow the Rule and Regulation on their Approach of worshipping Allah as Allah said in Surah 53 An-Najm 19. **Have you then considered Al-Lat, and Al- Uzza (two idols of the pagan Arabs) 20. And Manat (another idol of the pagan Arabs), the other third? 21. Is it for you the males and for Him the females? 22. That indeed is a division most unfair! 23. They are but names which you have named-- you and your fathers-- for which Allah has sent down no authority. They follow but a guess and that which they themselves desire, whereas there has surely, come to them the Guidance from their Lord! 24. Or shall man have what he wishes? 25. But to Allah belongs the last (Hereafter) and the first (the world).**

The 3 fundamental Rules of how we worship Allah is 1. Only Say about Allah what Allah says about himself and only worship him the way Allah tells us to worship him 2 Say about Allah what he revealed to any one of his prophets about himself and worship him the way those prophets show us that Allah revealed to them to worship him 3. Stop where Allah and his Messengers stopped (don't assume, used metaphorical, or say about Allah what we have no proof of). The Science of Tauhid can be broken down into 3 levels for the sake of understanding: 1. Tauhid Ar-Rububiyyah, 2. Tauhid Al-Uluhiyya, and 3. Tauhid Al-Asma Was-Sifat

Tauhid Ar-Rububiyyah

Oneness of the Lordship of Allah

Allah said in Surah 39 Az Zumar 62 **Allah is the Creator of all things, and He is the Wakil (Trustee, Disposer of affairs, Guardian) over all things. 63. To Him belong the keys of the heavens and the earth. And those who disbelieve in the Ayats (proofs, evidences,** verses, signs, revelations, etc.) of Allah, such are they who will be the losers.

Every one of Allah's creatures believe in the Oneness of Allah this Tauhid Ar- Rububiyyah, as

Allah said in Surah 3 Ali Imran 83. **Do they seek other than the religion of Allah, while to Him submitted all creatures willingly or unwillingly. And to Him shall they all be returned.**

Ahlul Kitab {the people of the Book {the torah and injil - the gospel)} believe in the Lordship of Allah and this is why The Prophet (may peace and blessing be upon him) as we call the people to Islam start with "La ilaha illallah"

It is reported on the authority of Ibn Abbas that Mu'ath said: The Messenger of Allah (may peace and blessing be upon him) had sent me (as a governor of Yemen) and (at the time of departure) instructed me thus: You will soon find yourself in a community of the people of the Book. So first call them to testify that there is no God but Allah, that I {(Muhammad (may peace and blessing be upon him)} am the Messenger of Allah, and if they accept this, then tell them that Allah has enjoined upon them five prayers during the day and the night and if they accept it, then tell them that Allah has made Zakat obligatory for them that it should be collected from the rich and distributed among the poor, and if they agree to it, don't pick up (as a share of Zakat) the best of their wealths. Beware of the supplication of the oppressed for there is no barrier between him and Allah.

Sahih Muslim
Book 1, p43, #19

The Pagans of the time of the Messenger of Allah (may peace and blessing be upon him) also believed in the one true God, the problem

17

is that they associated partnership with their worship. If we look at Ikrimah's (who was a pagan) conversion to Islam

Muhammad bin Ishaq reported from `Ikrimah bin Abi Jahl that when the Messenger of Allah conquered Makkah, he (`Ikrimah) ran away, fleeing from him. When he was on the sea, headed for Ethiopia, the ship started to rock and the crew said:

O people, pray sincerely to your Lord alone, for no one can save us from this except Him.

`Ikrimah said: By Allah, if there is none who can save us on the sea except Him, then there is none who can save us on land except Him either, O Allah, I vow to You that if I come out of this, I will go and put my hand in the hand of Muhammad and I will find him kind and merciful.

And this is what indeed did happen.

[Tabarani]

And if we look at the Treaty of Hudaybiya Suhayl ibn `Amr knew Allah

The Muslims demanded leave to enter Makkah by force, but he refused in order not to show disrespect for the Ka'bah. The Quraysh and the Muslims, finally agreed to sign a peace treaty. The Prophet (SA) dictated the peace treaty to `Ali (RA) who wrote it down. The Prophet (SA) ordered him to write: "In the name of Allah, the Beneficent, the Merciful." Suhayl ibn `Amr, representing the Quraysh, protested and said: "This is your slogan, with which we are not familiar. Write: `In your name, O Allah!"

The Prophet (SA) agreed and ordered `Ali (RA) to write accordingly. Then, the Prophet (SA) ordered him to write: "This is a contract being concluded between Muhammad, Allah's messenger and the Quraysh".

The representative for the Quraysh objected saying: "We do not regard you as Allah's messenger." Only your followers regard you likewise. If we had regarded you as Allah's messenger, we would not have fought against you, nor had barred your entry to Makkah. Write your and your father's name".

The Prophet (SA) said: "Whether or not you regard me as Allah's messenger, I am Allah's messenger".

Then, he ordered `Ali (RA) to write: "This is a treaty being concluded between Muhammad ibn `Abdillah and the people of Quraysh". It was at this point that the Muslims became angry. From this point on, the historical accounts differ in certain respects.

Ibn Hisham's "Sirat Ibn Hisham" and also from Sahih Al-Bukhari

Today we have those who claim to be Atheist and/or Agnostic yet as soon as a person gets to an excited state of being overjoyed or a calamity happens in their lives their natural inclination is to call out "Oh My God", Why Me Lord, Thank God. In Islam we attribute this to a natural Fitrah. "Fitra" or "fitrah" (Arabic: فطرة fiṭrah), is the state of purity and innocence Muslims believe all humans to be born with, comparable to the Latin term tabula rasa, in other words, a blank canvas. Fitra is an Arabic word that is usually translated as "original disposition," "natural constitution," or "innate nature."

According to Islamic theology, human beings are born with an innate inclination of tawhid (Oneness), which is encapsulated in the fitra along with compassion, intelligence, ihsan and all other attributes that embody the concept of humanity. It is for this reason that some Muslims prefer to refer to those who embrace Islam as reverts rather than converts, as it is believed they are returning to a perceived pure state.

Al-Tabari (may Allah have mercy on him) said in his Tafseer: Fitrah:

the deen (way or religion) of Allah. Al-Tabaris tafseer (commentary) of the aayah (interpretation of the meaning):Al-Nisa 4:119 **[Iblees said] and indeed I will order them to change the nature created by Allah.**

Concerning the aayah (interpretation of the meaning), Al-Room 30:30 **So set your face steadily and truly to the Faith: (establish) Allah's handiwork according to the pattern (fitrah) on which He has made mankind: no change (let there be) in the work (wrought) by Allah: that is the standard Religion: but most among mankind understand not.**

It was reported from some of the scholars of tafseer that the phrase the pattern (fitrah) on which He has made mankind means the design of Allah according to which He has created mankind.

This word (fitrah) was also mentioned in the hadeeth narrated by Abu Hurayrah who said: The Messenger of Allah (peace and blessings of Allaah be upon him) said: Five things are part of the fitrah: removing the pubic hair, circumcision, trimming the moustache, plucking the armpit hairs, and trimming the nails.

(Reported by al-jamaaah)

What is meant by these five things being part of the fitrah is that when they are done, this is in accordance with the natural pattern on which Allah made mankind and urged them to follow, so that they will be better and more perfect This is the ancient sunnah (way) which was followed by all the Prophets and which was enjoined by all the laws they brought. It is a natural and innate way.

Al-Shawkaani, Nayl al-Awtaar,
Baab Sunan al-Fitrah.

What goes against the Fitrah (natural way) is Darwin's Theory of Evolution. Simply put that Man has evolved from apes, and it all started from an Amoeba. The concept of Microevolution to Macroevolution and Natural Selection is in essence saying that the creation created itself.

Allah said in Surah 52 At Tur 35. **Were they created by nothing? Or were they themselves the Creators?**

Allah said in Surah 65 At Talaq 12. **It is Allah who has created seven heavens and of the earth the like thereof (i.e. Seven). His command descends between them (heavens and earth), that you may know that Allah has power over all things, and that Allah surrounds all thing in His Knowledge.**

Unlike the concept that man was created in sin, Muslims believe Man had a very noble creation. Allah created Adam with His hand and breathed into him his soul created by Him, and told His angels to prostrate to him.

Allah created Adam from dust, as He says

Surah 3 Ali 'Imran 59 **"Verily, the likeness of 'Eesa (Jesus) before Allah is the likeness of Adam. He created him from dust, then (He) said to him: 'Be!' — and he was".**

When Allah had completed the creation of Adam, He commanded the angels to prostrate to him, so they prostrated, except for Iblees, who was present but he refused and was too arrogant to prostrate to Adam:

Allah said in Surah 38 Sad 71-74 **"(Remember) when your Lord said to the angels: 'Truly, I am going to create man from clay. So when I have fashioned him and breathed into him (his) soul created by Me, then you fall down prostrate to him.' So the angels prostrated themselves, all of them, Except Iblees (Satan), he was proud and was one of the disbelievers".**

Then Allah told the angels that He was going to place Adam on earth and make generations after generations of his offspring, and Allah taught Adam all the names:

Allah Surah 2 al-Baqarah 30 **"And (remember) when your Lord said to the angels: 'Verily, I am going to place (mankind) generations after generations on earth'".**

Allah said in Surah 2 al-Baqarah 31 **"And He taught Adam all the names (of everything)"**

When Iblees refused to prostrate to Adam, Allah expelled him and cursed him: Allah said in Surah 38 Sad 77-78 **"(Allaah) said: 'Then get out from here; for verily, you are outcast. And verily, My Curse is on you till the Day of Recompense'"**

When Iblees knew of his fate, he asked Allah to give him respite until the Day of Resurrection:

Allah said in Saad 38:79-81 **"[Iblees (Satan)] said: 'My Lord! Give me then respite till the Day the (dead) are resurrected.' Allah said: 'Verily, you are of those allowed respite Till the Day of the time appointed'".**

When Allah granted him that, he declared war on Adam and his descendents, made disobedience attractive to them and tempted them to commit immoral actions:

Allah tells us in Surah 38 Sad 82-83 **"[Iblees (Satan)] said: 'By Your Might, then I will surely, mislead them all, Except Your chosen slaves amongst them (i.e. faithful, obedient, true believers of Islamic Monotheism).'"**

Allah created Adam, and from him He created his wife, and from their progeny He created men and women,

Allah said in Surah 4 al-Nisaa' 1 **"O mankind! Be dutiful to your Lord, Who created you from a single person (Adam), and from him**

(Adam) He created his wife [Hawwa (Eve)], and from them both He created many men and women".

Then Allaah caused Adam and his wife to dwell in Paradise, eating of the fruits of Paradise but He forbade them to eat from one tree:

Allah said in Surah 2 Al Baqarah 35 **"And We said: 'O Adam! Dwell you and your wife in the Paradise and eat both of you freely with pleasure and delight, of things therein as wherever you will, but come not near this tree or you both will be of the Zaalimoon (wrong-doers)'"**

Allah warned Adam and his wife against the Shaytaan,

Allah said in Surah 20 Ta-Ha 117 **"O Adam! Verily, this is an enemy to you and to your wife. So let him not get you both out of Paradise, so that you will be distressed"** Then the Shaytaan whispered to Adam and his wife, and tempted them to eat from the forbidden tree. Adam forgot and could not resist the temptation, so he disobeyed his Lord and ate from that tree:

Allah said in Surah 20 Ta-Ha 120-121 **"Then Shaytaan (Satan) whispered to him, saying: 'O Adam! Shall I lead you to the Tree of Eternity and to a kingdom that will never waste away?' Then they both ate of the tree, and so their private parts became manifest to them, and they began to cover themselves with the leaves of the Paradise for their covering. Thus did Adam disobey his Lord, so he went astray"**

Their Lord called to them and said

Allah said in Surah 7 al-A'raaf 22 **"Did I not forbid you that tree and tell you: Verily, Shaytaan (Satan) is an open enemy unto you?"**

When they ate from the tree, they regretted what they had done, and said:

Allah tells us in Al-A'raf 7:23 **"Our Lord! We have wronged ourselves. If You forgive us not, and bestow not upon us Your Mercy, we shall certainly be of the losers"**

The sin of Adam stemmed from desire, not from arrogance, hence Allaah guided him to repent and He accepted that from him:

Allah Said in Surah 2 al-Baqarah 37 **"Then Adam received from his Lord Words. And his Lord pardoned him (accepted his repentance). Verily, He is the One Who forgives (accepts repentance), the Most Merciful".**

This is the way for Adam and his descendents: whoever sins then repents sincerely, Allah will accept his repentance:

Allah said in Surah 42 Ash-Shura 25 **"And He it is Who accepts repentance from His slaves, and forgives sins, and He knows what you do".**

Then Allaah sent Adam and his wife, and Iblees, down to the earth, and He sent down Revelation to them and He sent the Messengers to them. So whoever believes will return back to Paradise and whoever disbelieves will enter Hell:

Allah said in Surah 2 al-Baqarah 38-39 **"We said: 'Get down all of you from this place (the Paradise), then whenever there comes to you Guidance from Me, and whoever follows My Guidance, there shall be no fear on them, nor shall they grieve. But those who disbelieve and belie Our Ayaat (proofs, evidences, verses, lessons, signs, revelations, etc.) — such are the dwellers of the Fire. They shall abide therein forever'".**

Allah said in Surah 7 al-A'raf 24 "**(Allah) said: 'Get down, one of you an enemy to the other [i.e. Adam, Hawwa, (Eve), and Shaytaan (Satan)]. On earth will be a dwelling place for you and an enjoyment for a time'.**

Allah is Able to do all things. He created Adam with no father or mother, and He created Hawwa from a Man with no mother, and He created 'Eesa from a mother with no father, and He created us from a father and a mother. Allah created Adam from dust, then He made his descendents from sperm,

Allah said in Surah 32 Al Sajdah 7-9 "**Who made everything He has created good and He began the creation of man from clay. Then He made his offspring from semen of despised water (male and female sexual discharge).**

Then He fashioned him in due proportion, and breathed into him the soul (created by Allah for that person); and He gave you hearing (ears), sight (eyes) and hearts. Little is the thanks you give!" let's look at how man is created in the womb, and the stages which he goes through, is a wondrous thing.

Allah mentioned in Surah 23 al-Mu'minoon 12-14] "**And indeed We created man (Adam) out of an extract of clay (water and earth). Thereafter We made him (the offspring of Adam) as a Nutfah (mixed drops of the male and female sexual discharge and lodged it) in a safe lodging (womb of the woman). Then We made the Nutfah into a clot (a piece of thick coagulated blood), then We made the clot into a little lump of flesh, then We made out of that little lump of flesh bones, then We clothed the bones with flesh, and then We brought it forth as another creation. So Blessed is Allah, the Best of creators**"

The Prophet (peace and blessings of Allaah be upon him) said: "Allah has appointed an angel over the womb. He says, 'O Lord, a drop of semen (nutfah); O Lord, a clot ('alaqah); O Lord, a little lump of flesh (mudghah).' Then if Allah wishes (to complete) its creation, the angel asks, (O Lord) male or female, wretched (doomed to Hell) or blessed (destined for Paradise)? How much will his provision be? And what will his lifespan be?' So that is written whilst (the child) is still in the mother's womb."

(Narrated by al-Bukhaari, 318) Allah honoured the children of Adam and subjugated for their benefit that which is in the heavens and on earth:

Allah said in Surah 31 Luqman 20 **"See you not (O men) that Allaah has subjected for you whatsoever is in the heavens and whatsoever is in the earth, and has completed and perfected His Graces upon you, (both) apparent (i.e. Islamic Monotheism, and the lawful pleasures of this world, including health, good looks) and hidden [i.e. one's faith in Allah (of Islamic Monotheism), knowledge, wisdom, guidance for doing righteous deeds, and also the pleasures and delights of the Hereafter in Paradise]?**

Allaah has distinguished and honoured man with reason by which he knows his Lord, Creator and Provider, and by which he knows what is good and evil, what will benefit him and what will harm him, what is halaal and what is haraam. Allaah did not create man and leave him alone with no path to follow. Rather, Allah revealed the Books and sent Messengers to guide mankind to the Straight Path. Allah created people with a natural inclination towards monotheism (Tawheed – belief in the Oneness of Allah). Every time they deviated from that, Allah sent a Prophet to bring them back to the Straight Path. The first of the Prophets was Adam and the last was Muhammad (peace and blessings of Allaah be upon them all):

Allah said Al-Baqarah 2:213 **"Mankind were one community**

and Allah sent Prophets with glad tidings and warnings, and with them He sent down the Scripture in truth to judge between people in matters wherein they differed

All the Messengers called people to the same truth, which is the worship of Allah alone and to reject all gods besides Him

Allah said in Surah An-Nahl 16:36 **"And verily, We have sent among every Ummah (community, nation) a Messenger (proclaiming): "Worship Allah (Alone), and avoid (or keep away from) Taaghoot (all false deities, i.e. do not worship Taaghoot besides Allah)."**

Tauhid Al- Uluhiyyah
Oneness of the worship of Allah

It is Narrated on the authority of Mu'ath B. Jabal: I was riding behind the Hold Prophet (may peace and blessing be upon him). There was nothing between him and me but the rear part of the saddle, when he said; Mu'ath B. Jabal: to which I replied: At your beck and call, and at your pleasure, Messenger of Allah (may peace and blessing be upon him)! He moved along for a few minutes, when again he said: Mu'ath B. Jabal. To which I replied: At your beck and call, and at your pleasure, Messenger of Allah (may peace and blessing be upon him)! He then again moved along for a few minutes and said: Mu'ath b. Jabal! To which I replied: At your beck and call, and at your pleasure, Messenger of Allah (may peace and blessing be upon him)! He {the Holy Prophet (may peace and blessing be upon him)} said: Do you Know what rights Allah has upon His servants? I said: Allah and His Messenger know better. He {the Holy Prophet (may peace and blessing be upon him)} said: Verily the right of Allah over His servants is that they should worship Him, not associating anything with Him.

He {the Holy Prophet (may peace and blessing be upon him)}, with Mu'ath behind him, moved along for a few minutes and said:Mu'ath b. Jabal! To which I replied: At your beck and call, and at your pleasure Messenger of Allah (may peace and blessing be upon him)! He (the Holy Prophet) remarked; That He would not torment to them (with the Fired of Hell).

Sahih Muslim
P. 52, book 1, #30

Allah said in Surah 17 Al Isra 23. **And your Lord has decreed that you worship none but him. And that you be dutiful to your parents.**

Allah said in Surah 39. AzZumar 65. **And indeed it has been revealed to you (O Muhammad), as it was to those before you: If you join others in worship with Allah, (then) surely, all your deeds will be in vain, and you will certainly be among the losers.**

It is narrated on the authority of Abu Malik: I heard the Messenger of Allah (may peace and blessing be upon him) saying: He who said that there is no God but Allah and did not believe in everything worshipped besides Allah, his property and blood became inviolate, and his affairs rest with Allah.

Sahih Muslim
Book 1, p. 47, #23

Rububiya (oneness of Lordship of Creation) is the 1st level or ground floor and reason we have this mission of understanding how to worship Allah. Due to the Fact that Allah has created us and created a world which can sustain our every need necessitates us to Move to Uluhiyyah (oneness of Lordship through Worship). This level on this journey to worshipping Allah can be considered the middle floor and the thing that should motivate us to want Ihsan (perfection in worship) by assuming we can we can see Allah but if we can not position our mind to this level of devotion at least we know Allah is seeing us. The Roof of this virtual building is Tauhid As-was-Sifat.

Tauhid Al Asma was- Sifat
Oneness of Lordship by his names and attributes

Allah said in Surah 7 Al- A'Raf 180 **And all the Most Beautiful names belong to Allah, So call on Him by them, and leave the company of those who belie or deny (or utter imious speech against) His names. They will be requite for what they used to do.**

Narrated Abu Hurairah (RA): Allah has ninety- nine names, i.e. one-hundred minus one; and whoever believes in their meanings and acts accordingly, will enter Paradise; and Allah is Witr (one) and loves the Witr.

Sahih Al Bukhari
Vol 8 #419 hadith on Surah 7: 180 in Noble

Allah said in Surah 18 Al- Kahf 110. {**O Muhammad (may peace and blessing be upon him)**} **Invoke Allah or invoke The Most gracious (Allah), by whatever name you invoke Him (it is the same), for to Him belong the Best Names. And offer your Salat (prayer) neither aloud nor in a low voice, but follow a way between.**

Allah said in Surah 87 Al- A'la 1 **Glorify the Name of your Lord, the Most High,**

There are some who think Allah only has 99 names but this is a misunderstanding. The reality is that Allah

has an infinite number of names and out of that infinite
number of name there is 99 that if we do *ihsaha* -believes
in their meanings and acts accordingly, will enter Paradise

Ibn Mas'ud reported: The Messenger of Allah, peace and blessings
be upon him, said, "If any Muslim is afflicted with distress and makes
this supplication, then his supplication will be answered: O Allah, I
am your servant, the son of your servant, the son of your maidservant.
My forelock is in your hand, your command concerning me prevails,
and your decision concerning me is just. I call upon you by every one of
the beautiful names with which you have described yourself, or which
you have revealed in your Books, or you have taught to anyone of your
creatures, or which you have chosen to keep in the knowledge of the
unseen with you, to make the Quran the delight of my heart, the light of
my chest, and to remove my sadness and dispel my anxiety." The Prophet
said, "If he says this, Allah will remove his affliction and replace it with
joy and happiness." They said, "O Messenger of Allah, should we not
learn it?" The Prophet said, "Yes, whoever hears it should know it."

Musnad Ahmad 3704

Allah said in Surah 59 Al- Hashr 22. **He is Allah whom La ilaha ila
huwa (none has the right to be worshipped but He) The All-Knower of
the unseen and the seen. He is Most Gracious, The Most Merciful. 23.
He is Allah whom La ilaha ila huwa (none has the right to be worshipped
but He) The King, The Holy, The One Free from all defects, The Giver
of Security, The Compeller, The Supreme. Glory is to Allah! (High is
He) above all that they associate as partners with Him. 24. He is Allah,
The Creator, The Inventor of all things, The Bestower of Forms. To
Him belong the Best Names. All that is in the heavens and the earth
glorify him. And He is the All- Mighty, The All- Wise.**

Salaat

Salaat is the second pillar of Islam and Allah tells us to establish Salaat and remain steadfast in your prayers.

Allah said in Surah 20 TaHa 130 **Therefore be patient with what they say and celebrate constantly the praise of thy Lord before the rising of the sun and before its setting; Yea, celebrate them for part of the hours of the night, and at the sides of the day: that thou mayest have spiritual joy.**

The prayer before Sunrise is clearly Fajr; that before sunset is Asr; Part of the hours of the night would indicate Maghrib and Isha. Thuhr is the indefinite side or middle of the day.

Narrated Malik bin Sa sa'ah(ra): The Prophet (may peace and blessings be upon him) said, "While I was at the house in a state midway between sleep and wakefulness an Angel recognized me as the man lying between two men. A golden tray full of wisdom and belief was brought to me and my body was cut open from the throat to the lower part of the abdomen and then my abdomen was washed with Zam zam water and my heart was filled with wisdom and belief. Al-Buraq, a white animal smaller than a mule and bigger than a donkey was brought to me and I set out with Jibriel. When I reached the nearest heaven, Jabriel said to the gatekeeper of heaven, 'Open the gate'. The gatekeeper asked 'who is it?' He said 'Jabriel'. The gatekeeper said, 'who is accompanying you?' Jabriel said Muhammad (may peace and blessing be upon him). The gatekeeper said, Has he been called?" Jibriel said, Yes. Then it was said "He is welcome. What a wonderful visit this is! Then I met Adam (AS) and greeted him and he said, 'You are welcome O son and a Prophet'. Then we ascended to the second heaven. It was asked, 'Who is it?' Jabriel said, 'Jabriel', it was said, 'Who is with you?' he said, Muhammad (may peace and blessing be upon him). It was asked, has he been sent for?' he said 'Yes". It was said, He is welcome. What a wonderful visit this is! Then I met Isa[(Jesus) as] and Yahya [(John) as] who said, 'You are welcome, O brother and Prophet'. Then we ascended to the third heaven. It was asked, 'who is it?' Jabriel said, 'Jabriel'. It was asked, 'Who is with you?' Jabriel said, Muhammad (may peace and blessing be upon him). It was asked, 'Has he been sent for?' Jabriel said, 'yes'. It was said, 'He is welcome, what a wonderful visit this is! The Prophet (may peace and blessing be upon him) added: There I met Yusuf [(Joseph)as] and greeted him and he replied, 'You are welcome. O brother and Prophet! Then we ascended to the fourth heaven and again the same questions and answers were exchanged as in the previous heavens. There I met Idris [(enoch) as] and greeted him. He said, 'you are welcome, O brother and Prophet.' Then we ascended to the fifth heaven and again the same questions and answers were exchanged as in the previous heavens. There I met and greeted Harun[(Aaron)as] who said, 'You are welcome, O brother and a Prophet.' Then we ascended to the sixth heaven and again the same questions and answers were exchanged as in the previous heavens, There I met and greeted Musa [(Moses)as] who said, 'You are welcome, O brother and a Prophet'. When I proceeded on he started weeping and on being asked why he was weeping, he said, 'O Lord! Followers of this youth who was sent after me, will enter Paradise in greater numbers than my followers'. Then we ascended to the seventh heaven and again the same questions and answers were exchanged as in the previous heavens. There I met and greeted Ibrahim [(Abraham)as] who said. 'You are welcome, O son and a Prophet'. Then I was shown Al- Bait al Ma'mur (Allah's House). I asked Jabriel about it and he said, 'This is Al-Bait Al- Ma'Mur where 70,000 angels perform prayers daily; and when they leave they never return to it (but always a fresh batch comes into it daily)'. Then I was shown Sidat ul- Muntah (the lote tree of the utmost boundary over the seventh heaven) and I saw it's Nabiq fruits which resembled the clay jugs of Hijar (a town in Arabia) and it's leaves were like the ears of elephants, and four rivers originated at its root:two of them were apparent and two were hidden. I asked Jabriel about those rivers and he said, 'The two hidden rivers are in Paradise and the apparent ones are the Nile and the Euphrates'.

Then fifty prayers were enjoined on me. I descended till I met Musa(as) who asked me,' What had you done?' I said 'Fifty prayers have been enjoined on me'. He said, 'I know the people better than you, because I had the hardest experience to bring Bani Israel to obedience. Your followers cannot put up with such obligations. So, return to your Lord and request Allah for reduction and he made them forty. I returned and met Musa (AS) and had a similar discussion, and then returned to Allah for reduction and He made them thirty, then twenty, then ten; and then I came to musa (AS) who repeated the same advice. Ultimately Allah reduced them to five. When I came to Musa (AS) again, he said 'What have you done?'I said, "Allah has made them five only'. He repeated the same advice but I said that I surrendered to Allah's final order'. Allah's Messenger (may peace and blessing be upon him) was addressed by Allah: "I have decreed my obligation and have reduced the burden on my slaves, and I shall reward a single good as if it were ten good deeds".

Sahih Al-Bukhari 4/3207 (O.P. 429)

Abd Allah Ibn Mas'ud is reported to have asked the Holy Prophet (may peace and blessing be upon him) which deed is the dearest to God? The Messenger of Allah (may peace and blessing be upon him) replied: to offer the prayer at their due times. I asked: 'What is the next?' He replied: To be good and dutiful to your parents. I asked again: 'What is the next?' He replied: To strive in the way of Allah.

Sahih Al-Bukhari 2630

Sahih Muslim 85

Graded Muttafaqun Alayhi (authenticity agreed upon)

According to Al-Bukhari and Muslim

Allah said in Surah 2 Al-Baqarah 1. **Alif Lam Mim 2. This is the Book; In it is Guidance sure, without doubt to those who fear Allah:3. Who believe in the unseen, and steadfast in prayer, and spend out of what we have provided for them 4. And who believe in the revelation sent to thee, and sent before thy time, and in their hearts have the assurance of the Hereafter. 5. They are on true guidance, from their Lord, and it is these who will prosper.**

Allah said in Surah 2 Al Baqarah 42. **And cover not truth with falsehood, nor conceal the truth when ye know what it is. 43. And be steadfast in prayer; Practise regular charity; and bow down your heads with those who bow down in worship 44. Do ye enjoin right conduct on the people and forget to practise it yourselves. And yet ye study the scripture? Will ye not understand? 45. Nay, Seek Allah's help with patient perseverance and prayer: It is indeed hard, except to those who bring a lowly spirit. 46. Who bear in mind the certainty that they are to meet their Lord, and that they are to return to him.**

Each and every Muslim, male and female, is obliged to offer his/her salaat regularly five times a day at specified times; the male in the mosque in congregation and as for the female it is best to offer them at home.

As the Prophet (may peace and blessing be upon him) said: "Order your children to perform Salaat at the age of Seven and beat them about it at the age of 10yrs old.

Abu Dawood 459 and Ahmad 6650

Abu Hurayra (RA) is reported to have said: Had the people known what is in the call to prayer and in the first row, they would have drawn lots for it. And if they had known what is the reward for the midday prayer they would have raced for it. And if they had known the reward for the night and dawn prayers in congregation they would have joined them even if they are led to crawl.

Sahih Muslim p. 48 #41

The Messenger of Allah (may peace and blessing be upon him) is reported to have said: The congregational prayer is better than the prayer offered alone by twenty five times.

Sahih Muslim p55

We should know that we are strongly suggested as Men to pray in congregation in the mosque and women are suggested to pray in the home, however issues may arise when a man must pray the five AsSalaawats in his home. The Sunnah Prayers are already suggested to pray in the home. During a plagues such as Thatal AnWaat during the time of Rusullullah and the present CoronaVirus/ Covid 19 we are suggested to quarantine yourself as much as possible to prevent the spread of the illness to each other.

Jabir (RA) is reported to have said that the Messenger of Allah (may peace and blessing be upon him) said: Establish your prayer in the mosque but offer some of your prayers at home, as God Almighty blesses the house in which prayer is offered.

Sahih Muslim 60 #103

Allah said in Surah 17 Al-Isra 106. **It is a Quran which we have divided into parts from time to time, in order that thou mightest recite it to men at intervals: We have revealed it by stages. 107. Say: Whether ye believe in it or not, it is true that those who were given knowledge beforehand, when it is recited to them Fall down on their faces in humble prostration, 108. And they say: Glory To our Lord! Truly had the promise of our Lord been fulfilled! 109. They fall down on their faces in tears, and it increases their earnest humility 110. Say: "Call upon Allah, or call upon Rahman: By whatever name ye call upon him, it is well for to him belong the Most Beautiful Names. Neither Speak thy prayer aloud, nor speak it in a low tone, but seek a middle course between".**

Abu Hurayra (RA) is reported to have related that Abu Jahl said: Are you going to permit Muhammad to prostrate upon the dust in front of you? They said: "Yes". He said: "By Lat and by Uzza, if I see him do so, I shall put my foot on his neck or I shall wipe his face in the dusk". He went to the Messenger of Allah (may peace and blessing be upon him) while he was praying intending to stand on his neck but they were surprised to see Abu Jahl turning back upon his heels in fright, Trying to protect himself with his hands, They asked him: 'What happened to you?' He replied: I found between him and me a trench of Hell Fire and a terrifying thing with wings'. So Allah, Most Exalted revealed: 'No indeed, mankind is surely ever insolent, for he deems himself self-sufficient. Surely to your Lord is the return. Have you seen he who forbids the servant of God when he prays, have you considered if he were guided, or enjoined piety? Have you seen if he denies the Truth and turns away? Does he not realize that God sees all? No indeed, if he does not desist, We shall drag him by the forelock, a lying sinful forelock, let him then call his henchmen, we shall call the guards of Hell. No indeed, never obey him'. Surah 96: 6-19).

Sahih Muslim 277, #14

It was related that Uthman Ibn Abu Al-As said:" I went to the Messenger of Allah (may peace and blessing be upon him) and said: 'O Messenger of God (may peace and blessing be upon him), Satan disturbs my prayer and my recitation of the Qur'an and confuses me'. The Messenger of God (may peace and blessing be upon him) said: 'That is the work of he who is known as Khinzab, and when you feel it, seek refuge in God from it three times and spit three times to your left side. "I did so and God warded it away from me.

Sahih Muslim

P.257, #6

Abd Allah Ibn Mas'ud reported that a man came to the apostle of Allah (may peace and blessing be upon him) and said: 'O Messenger of Allah (may peace and blessing be upon him)! I have unlawfully kissed a woman at the reaches of Madina and all I did was kiss her. So here I am, pass judgement upon me as you deem appropriate'. Umar (RA) said: 'Allah has covered you so why do you not cover yourself?' The Prophet (may peace and blessing be upon him) did not reply. So the man left and the Messenger of Allah (may peace and blessing be upon him) sent a man to call him back, then he recited to him:' And establish regular prayers at the two ends of the day and when night approaches, surely the good deeds blot out the evil deeds. This is a reminder for those who remember Allah'. (Surah 11 Hud: 114) A man asked: O messenger of Allah (may peace and blessing be upon him) is that just for him? He (may peace and blessing be upon him) said: 'It's for all my followers'.

Khushu in Salaat

Imaam Shafa'i said "All humans are dead except those who have knowledge; and all those who have knowledge are asleep except those who do good deeds; and those who do good deeds are deceived except those who are sincere and always in a state of worry.

Allah said in Surah 107 Al Maa'un **1. Have you seen him who denies the recompense? 2. That is he who repulses the orphan (harshly). 3. And urges not on the feeding of Al-Miskin (the poor), 4. So woe unto those performers of Salaat (prayer)/(Hypocrites). 5. Those who delay their Salaat (prayer from their stated fixed times). 6. Those who do good deeds only to be seen of men, 7. And with hold Al-Ma'un (small kindnesses)**

Narrated Abu Hurairah (RA): Allah's Messenger (may peace and blessing be upon him) entered the mosque and a person followed him. The man offered Salaat (prayer) and went to the Prophet (may peace and blessing be upon him) and greeted him. The Prophet (may peace and blessing be upon him) returned the greeting and said to go back and offered the Salaat (prayer) for you have not offered Salaat (prayer). The man went back, offered Salaat (prayer) in the same way as before and returned and greeted the Prophet (may peace and blessing be upon him) who said, "Go back and offer Salaat (prayer) for you have not offered Salat (prayer)". This happened thrice.

The man said, "By Him who sent you with the Truth, I cannot offer the Salaat(prayer) in a better way than this. Please teach me how to offer Salaat (prayer). The Prophet (may peace and blessing be upon him) said,

"When you stand for Salaat (prayer) say Takbir and then recite from the Quran (of what you know by heart) and then bow till you feel at ease. Then raise your head and stand up straight, them prostrate till you feel at ease during your prostration, then sit with calmness till you feel at ease (do not hurry) and do the same in all your Salaat (prayer)".

Sahih Al Bukhari

1. Successful indeed are the believers 2. Those who offer their Salaat (prayers) with all solemnity and full submissiveness.

Allah also said in this same Surah 23 Al Mu'minun 9. **And those who strictly guard their five compulsory congregational AsSalawat (prayers).**

Anas B Malik (RA) said: I did not offer prayer behind anyone more brief then the one offered by the Apostle of Allah (may peace and blessing be upon him) and that was perfect. When the Apostle of Allah (may peace and blessing be upon him) said: "Allah listens to him who praises him", he stood so long that we thought that he had omitted something; then two prostration so long that we thought that he had omitted something.

Sunnah Abu Dawud This tradition shows that the Prophet (may peace and blessing be upon him) would observe bowing, prostration, standing after bowing and sitting between prostrations for a long duration, but his prayer would be brief and perfect for his recite short surahs in the prayer and did not make haste in the observance of bowing and prostrating.

Narrated Jabir bin Abdullah (RA):Mu'adh bin Jabal (RA) used to offer Salaat (prayer) with the Prophet (may peace and blessing be upon him) and then go to lead his people in Salaat (prayer). Once he led the people in Salaat (prayer) and recited Surah Al Baqarah. A man left (the row of the people offering Salaat) and offered a light Salaat (prayer) separately and went away. When Mu'adh came to know about it he said, "He (that man) is a hypocrite". Later, that man heard what Mu'adh said about him, so he came to the Prophet (may peace and blessing be upon him) and said, O Allah's Messenger (may peace and blessing be upon him)! we are people who work with our own hands and irrigate (our farms) with our Camels. Last night Mu'adh let us in the night Salaat (prayer) and he recited Surah Al Baqarah, so I offered my prayer separately, and because of that, he accused me of being a hypocrite". The Prophet (may peace and blessing be upon him) called Mu'adh and said thrice, "O Mu'adh! You are putting the people to trails? Recite, Wash-shamsi wad-duhaha (Surah # 91) or the like ".

Sahih Al Bukhari The Prophet (may peace and blessings be upon him) recommended to Mu'adh that he should recite short Surahs when he is leading the people in congregation.

Allah commanded us to Pray on time in Surah 2 Al Baqarah 238. **Guard strictly (five obligatory) AsSalawat (the prayers) especially the middle Salaat (the best prayer Asr) and stand before Allah with obedience.**

Salat is a sign of a believer as

Allah said in Surah 9 At- Taubah 71. **The believers, men and women, are Auliya (helpers, supports, friends protectors) of one another; they enjoin on the people Al Ma'ruf (Islamic Monotheism and all that Islam orders one to do), and forbid people from Al-Munkar (Polytheism and disbelief of all kinds, and all that Islam has forbidden); they perform As Salaat (Iqamat-as-Salaat), and give the Zakaat, and obey Allah and His Messenger. Allah will have His mercy on them. Surely, Allah is All- Mighty, All- Wise.**

Allah's help come from Salaat:

Allah said in Surah 2 Al Baqarah 45. **And seek help in Patience and As Salaat (the prayer) and truly, it is extremely heavy and hard except for Al-Khashi'un (the true believers in Allah - those who obey Allah with Full Submission, fear much from His Punishment, and believe in His Promise {Paradise} and in His Warning {Hell}).**

Surah 2 Al Baqarah 153 **O you who Believe! Seek help in patience and As- Salaat (the prayer). Truly, Allah is with As-Sabirun (the patient).**

Shayton tries to distract you from the benefits of As Salaat as

Allah said in Surah 5 Al Ma'idah 91 **Shaitan (Satan) wants only to excite enmity and hatred between you with intoxicants and gambling, and hinder you from the remembrance of Allah and from As Salaat (the prayer). So will you not then abstain?**

Of those benefits is that those who perform As Salaat will have no fear on the Day of Judgement as

Allah said in Surah 2 Al Baqarah 277. **Truly, those who believe, and do deeds of righteousness, and perform As Salaat (Iqamat-as-Salaat), and give Zakat, they will have their reward with their Lord. On them shall be no fear, nor shall they grieve.**

Khushu means calmness and tranquility of the body and attentiveness of the mind, in Salaat. Loving the prayer and rushing to perform it with Khushu, and perfection inwardly and outwardly, demonstrates the heart's love for Allah and eagerness to meet him. On the other hand, disinterest in the prayer, Laziness in Answering the Adhan, and performing it alone, away from the congregation of Muslim in the Masjid, without a valid excuse, are all indications that the heart is empty of Allah's Love and disinterest in what he has with him.

Narrated Aishah (RA): I asked Allah's Messenger (may peace and blessing be upon him) about looking hither and thither in As Salaat (the prayer). He (may peace and blessing be upon him) replied, "It is a way of stealing by which Satan takes away a portion from the Salaat (prayer) of a person.

Sahih Al Bukhari 751

Abu Huraira reported that Allah's Messenger (may peace and blessing be upon him) had said: Do you know who is the Poor? They (the companions of the Holy Prophet {may peace and blessing be upon him}) said: "The poor amongst us is the one who has neither dirham with him nor wealth". He (may peace and blessing be upon him) said: The poor of my nation would be he who would come on The Day of Resurrection with prayer and fasts and pays Zakat but he would find himself bankrupt on that day as he would have exhausted his funds of virtues since he hurled abuse upon others, brought calumny and against others and unlawfully consumed the wealth of others and shed the blood of others and beat others, and his virtues would be credited to the account of one who suffered at the hand, and if his good deeds fall short to clear the account and he would be thrown in the Hell- Fire.

Sahih Muslim 2581

The Night Prayer

Tahajjad is the night optional prayer offered at any time after Isha prayer and before Fajr. Witr is an odd number of Rak'at with which one finishes Salaat (prayer) at night after the night prayer (Tahajjad) or Isha Prayer.

As Jabir is Reported to have related that the Messenger of Allah (may peace and blessing be upon him) said: "The one who fears he may miss the end of the night should offer his Witr Prayer at the beginning of the night, and the one who hopes to offer Witr Prayer at the end of the night, let him do so, as the prayer of the pre- dawn is witnesses, and that is better for you".

Sahih Muslim p.62, 116

Both Tahajjad and Witr are extra prayers known as Nawafal, which are optional practice of worship in contrast to obligatory (Faridah), used for spiritual advancement.

As Allah said in Surah 73 Muzzammil 1. **O thou folded in garments! 2. Stand to prayer by night, but not all night 3. Half of it or a little less, 4. Or a little more; and recite the Qur'an in slow measured rhythmic tones 5. Soon shall we send down to thee a weighty message.6. Truly the rising by night is most potent for governing the soul, and the word of prayer and praise.**

Al Mughira ibn Shu'adah is reported to have related that the Prophet (may peace and blessing be upon him) used to stand in prayer until both his feet or legs were swollen. He was asked why and he replied:" Should I not be a thankful servant.

Sahih Muslim p.279, #21

Allah said in Surah 39 Al Zumar 9. **Is one who is devoutly obedient during periods of the night, prostrating and standing [in prayer], fearing the Hereafter and hoping for the mercy of his Lord, [like one** who does not]? Say, "Are those who know equal to those who do not know?" Only they will remember [who are] people of understanding.

Narrated Ali Bin Abi Talib (RA) that one night Allah's Messenger (may peace and blessing be upon him) came to him and Fatima, the daughter of the Prophet (may peace and blessing be upon him), and said, "Don't you both offer the tahajjud prayer at night?" Ali (RA) said, 'O Allah's Messenger (may peace and blessing be upon him), our souls are in the hands of Allah (Mighty and Exalted is he) and if he wants us to get up he will make us get up'. When I said that, he (may peace and blessing be upon him) left us without saying anything and I heard that he was hitting his thigh and saying, "But man is more quarrelsome than anything".

Sahih Al Bukhari p.302#593

Narrated Abu Hurairah (RA): the Prophet (may peace and blessings be upon him) said, Allah said, I am just as my slave thinks I am, and I am with him if he remembers me. If he remembers me in himself, I to remember him in myself; and if he remembers me in a group of people, I remember him in a group that is better than them; and if he comes one span nearer to me, I go one cubit nearer to him; and if he comes one cubit nearer to me, I go a distance of two outstretched arms nearer to him; and if he come to me walking, I go to him running.

Sahih Al Bukhari
Hadith associated with Surah 2:152
In the Noble Quran

We all need to ask ourselves if calling ourselves Muslim is enough, doing the bear minimum but expecting the Greatest of Rewards.

It is reported from Talha ibn Ubaydallah (RA) that a man from Najd approached the Messenger of Allah (may peace and blessing be upon him), and enquired about the essential duties to be performed in Islam.

The Holy Prophet (may peace and blessing be upon him) replied: You have to establish prayer 5 times over the course of a day and night. The man asked: Are there any other prayers due? The Great Teacher (may peace and blessing be upon him) replied: No but you may offer voluntary prayers, and you have to fast during the month of Ramadan. The man asked: Is there any other fasting due? The Messenger of Allah (may peace and blessing be upon him) replied: No but you may offer Voluntary fasting. The Apostle of Allah (may peace and blessing be upon him) then said to him: You have to give Zakat (the obligatory poor due). The man asked: Is there any other charity due? The Great Seer (may peace and blessing be upon him), observed: No, but you may offer voluntary charity. As the man was leaving the man said: By God! I will do neither more nor less than that! The Holy Prophet (may peace and blessing be upon him) said: If he does as he says, then he will be successful.

Sahih Muslim p. 12#38

We can be successful if we complete only the basic essentials and offering none of the voluntary/optional practices of worship, however the person who offers all five AsSalaawats on time, Fast the whole month of Ramadan, Gives the prescribed Zakaat will be successful but can he not also be a Thankful Servant. Is there anything that we would like to be forgiven for, or something we need to ask for, or are we without sin?

'Abu Hurayra (RA) is reported to have related that the Holy Prophet (may peace and blessing be upon him)said: by the One is whose hand is my soul, had you not committed sin, Allah would get rid of you and place you with another people who would sin, and then they would seek Allah's Forgiveness, so he would forgive them.

Sahih Muslim 2749

Allah said in Surah 51 Al Dhariyat 15. **As to the righteous, they will be in the midst of Gardens and Springs,16. Taking joy in the things which the Lord gives them, because before then, they lived a good life. 17. They were in the habit of sleeping but little by night, 18. And in the hours of early dawn, they were found praying for forgiveness.**

It has been reported on the Authority of Abu Hurayra (RA) that the Apostle of Allah (may peace and blessing be upon him) said: Whoever seeks Forgiveness before the rising of the sun from the west, God will turn to him with mercy.

Sahih Muslim p.347,#1

Jabir is reported to have said that he heard the Apostle of Allah (may peace and blessing be upon him) say that there is an hour in the night in which if any muslim asked Allah for something good for this life or the hereafter Allah will grant it to him. And it is in every night.

Sahih Muslim p.61#113

Allah said in Surah 73 Al Muzzammil 20. **Thy Lord doth know that thou standest forth to prayer nigh two-thirds of the night, or half the night, or a third of the night, and so doth a party of those with thee. But Allah doth apoint Night and Day in due measure. He knoweth that ye are unable to keep count thereof. So he hath turned to you in mercy: read ye, therefore, of the Quran as much as may be easy for you. He knoweth that there may be some among you in ill health; others travelling through the land, seeking of Allah's bounty; yet others fighting in Allah's cause. Read ye therefore, as much of the Qur'an as may be easy for you.**

The way I feel when I offer Salat is relieved, refreshed, Clean, Righteous and blessed. First I brush my teeth and offer a wuthu and say my Du'a. I Call the Athan and give my family about 15-20 minutes to prepare for the prayer. Some offer du'a, read the Qur'an or offer Sunnah's prayers during this time. Then I Call the Ikaamah, make sure everybody is Lined up straight and tight (Foot{heal} to foot{Heal} and shoulder to shoulder). Then I raise my hands and say "Allahu Akbar". I say the du'a to begin prayer the prayer. We must realize that The Messenger of Allah (may peace and blessings be upon him) shows us many different Du'as all throughout his Salat for different reasons and we need to learn the bare minimum and add to it throughout our lives. I then recite the Al-Fatihah (The Opening {the 7 oft- repeated verses}) which contain a Du'a in itself where we ask Allah to "Guide us to the straight path" and because of this Du'a we all say "Ameen". It is mentioned, "When the imam says 'Ameen' then say 'Ameen,' for if a person's saying Ameen coincides with that of the angels, his previous sins will be forgiven" Narrated by al-Bukhaari (780) and Muslim (410). I then recite from the Qur'an what comes easy to me. I say Allahu Akbar then bow in a way that my back is completely straight (in a 90 degree angle) and allow my bones to come to rest. While bowing i do what considered Ruf Al-yadayn - Raising my Hand to my chest with my utterance "Allahu Akbar". Narrated by al-Bukhaari (735) and Muslim (390) from 'Abd- Allaah ibn 'Umar (may Allah be pleased with them both), who said that the Messenger of Allah (peace and blessings of Allaah be upon him) used to raise his hands to shoulder level when he started to pray, when he said "Allahu akbar" before bowing in rukoo', and when he raised his head from rukoo'. I raise up with "Sami'a Allaahu liman hamidah" and everyone will respond "Allaahumma Rabbana wa laka'l-hamd." Narrated Abu Hurayrah (may Allah be pleased with him) said: "When the Messenger of Allaah (peace and blessings of Allaah be upon him) said Sami'a Allaahu liman hamidah, he would say Allaahumma Rabbana wa laka'l-hamd." Narrated by al-Bukhaari (795) and Muslim (392). Then I prostrate with Ruf Al-Yadayn and say the appropriate du'a taking my time in each prostration and then raise to begin the next Rakat. During my prayer I focus my eyes on my place of prostration and I finish my prayer sitting saying the appropriate du'a. It was narrated that the Prophet (peace and blessings of Allaah be upon him) said to a man: "What do you say when you pray?" He said: "I recite the tashahhud, then I say: Allaahumma inni as'aluka al-jannah wa a'oodhu bika min al-naar (O Allah, I ask You for Paradise and seek refuge in You from the Fire). I cannot murmur like you and like Mu'aadh." The Prophet (peace and blessings of Allaah be upon him) said: "It is about them that we were murmuring." Narrated by Abu Dawood, 792; classed as saheeh by al- Albaani in Saheeh Abi Dawood. I finish the prayer giving Salaams to the right and the left. I say Astigfirallah three times for any mistakes I may have made during this prayer and then say Ayatal Kursy Surah 2:255, dhikr, and beg Allah for forgiveness, supplicate to Allah, and beg Allah for what I want.

Sadaqah

A Beautiful Loan

Allah Said in Surah 57 Al Hadid 10. **And what is the matter with you that you spend not in the cause of Allah? And to Allah belongs the heritage of the heavens and earth. Not equal among you are those who spent and fought before the conquering of Makkah with those among you who did so later. Such are high in degree than those who spent and fought afterwards. But to all Allah has promised the best reward. And Allah is All-Aware of what you do.11. Who is he that will lend to Allah a goodly loan: then Allah will increase it manifold to his credit in repaying, and he will have besides a good reward (i.e. Paradise).**

In these verses Allah speaks about the companions of the Messenger of Allah (may peace and blessing be upon him) who spent and fought in the way of Allah. They are Degrees higher than the Muslims of today,

Allah said in Surah 9 Taubah 100. **And foremost to embrace Islam of the Muhajirun (those who migrated from Makkah to Al- Madinah) and the Ansar (the citizens of Al-Madinah who helped and gave aid to the Muhajirun) and also those who followed them as them exactly in faith, Allah is well pleased with them as they are well- pleased** with him. He has prepared for them Gardens under which rivers flow (Paradise), to dwell therein forever. That is the Supreme success.

Allah said in Surah 8 Al- Anfal 74. **And those who believed, and emigrated and stove hard in the cause of Allah (Al Jihad) as well as those who gave them Asylum and aid -- Those are believers in Truth, for them is Forgiveness and `*Rizqun Karim* (a generous provision i.e. Paradise).**

So the Truth in Faith, 1. Believe 2. Emigrate from our *Jahileeya* (Days of ignorance) and 3. Strive hard in the cause of Allah, with the understanding of those companions (*RadyiAllahu Anhu*) of the prophet (may peace and blessing be upon him) that Allah spoke about in these two ayats as well as many others. The scholars dispute whether Allah's statement "Not equal among you are those who spent and fought before the conquering" refers to the conquering of Makkah or the treaty at Al- Hudaybiyyah.

Anas, collected by Imam Ahmad, Anas said Khalid bin Al-Walid and Abdur Rahman bin Awf had a dispute. Khalid Said to Abdur Rahman, You boast about days (Battles) that you participated in before us.' When the news of this statement reached the Prophet (may peace and blessing be upon him) he said, do not bother my Companions, for by Him in whose Hand is my soul! If you spend an amount of gold equal to Mount Uhud, you will not reach the level of their actions.

Ahmad 3:266

Tafsir Ibn Kathir p. 473

Allah said in Surah 2 Al-Baqarah 245. **Who is he that will lend to Allah a goodly loan so that He may multiply it to him many times? And it is Allah that decreases or increases (your provisions), and unto Him you shall return.**

Allah said in Surah 2 Al-Baqarah 261. **The likeness of those who** spend their wealth in the way of Allah, is as the likeness of a grain of corn; it grows seven ears, and each ear has a hundred grains. Allah gives manifold increase to whom He wills. And Allah is All-Sufficient for His Creatures needs All- Knower.

Allah said in Surah 65 At-Talaq 17. **If you lend to Allah a goodly loan (i.e. spend in Allah's Cause), He will double it for you, and will forgive you. And Allah is Most Ready to appreciate and to reward, Most Forbearing, 18. All-Knower of the unseen and seen, the All-Mighty, the All-Wise.**

Allah said in Surah 57 Al-Hadid 18. **Very, those who give Sadaqat (i.e. Zakat and alms), men and women, and lend to Allah a goodly loan, it shall be increased manifold to their credit, and theirs shall be an honourable good reward (i.e. Paradise).**

Narrated Abu Hurairah (*RadyiAllahu Anhu*): Allah's Messenger (may peace and blessing be upon him) said, If one gives in charity what equals one date- fruit from the honestly earned money and Allah accepts only the honestly earned money- Allah takes it in His Right Hand and then enlarges its reward for that person who has given it, as anyone of you brings up his baby horse, so much so that it becomes as a mountain".

Sahih Al- Bukhari

Vol. 2 p. 286, #1410

Allah said in Surah 23 Al- Mu'minun 57. **Verily, those who live in awe for fear of their Lord; 58. And those who believe in the Ayat (proofs, evidence, verses, lessons, signs, revelations etc.) of their Lord; 59. And those who join not anyone in worship as partners with their Lord 60. And those who give that charity which they give and also do other good deeds with their hearts full of fear (whether their alms and charities have been accepted or not), because they are sure** to return to their Lord for reckoning. 61. It is those who hasten in the good deeds, and they are foremost in them [e.g. Offering the compulsory salaat (prayers) in their (early) stated, fixed times and so on].

Allah said in Surah 9 At-Taubah 102. **And there are others who have acknowledged their sins, they have mixed a deed that was righteous with another that was evil Perhaps Allah will turn unto them is forgiveness Surely, Allah is Oft- Forgiving, Most Merciful. 103. Take Sadaqah (alms) from their wealth in order to purify them and sanctify the, with it, and invoke Allah for them. Verily, your invocations are a source of security for them and Allah is All- Hearer, All- Knower(AsSamee'an Aleem). 104. Know they not that Allah accepts repentance from His slaves and takes the Sadaqat (alms, Charity), and that Allah alone is the One who Forgives and accepts repentance; Most Merciful?**

Narrated Abi bin Hatim ((*RadyiAllahu Anhu*)): I heard the Prophet (may peace and blessings be upon him) saying: "Save yourself from Hell- Fire even by giving half a date - fruit in charity".

Sahih Al Bukhari
Book #2 p. 289, #1417

Narrated Abdullah bin Abu Aufa ((*RadyiAllahu Anhu*)): whenever a person brought his alms to the Prophet (may peace and blessing be upon him) would say, "O Allah! Send your blessings upon so-and-so. My Father went to the Prophet (may peace and blessing be upon him) with his alms and the Prophet (may peace and blessing be upon him) said, "O Allah! Send your blessings upon the offspring of Abu Aufa".

Sahih Al Bukhari
Book#2 p.335, #1497

Abu Tharr reported: Some of the Companions of the Apostle of Allah (may peace and blessing be upon him) said to him: Messenger of Allah (may peace and blessing be upon him), the rich have taken all the rewards. They observe prayer as we do; they keep the pasts as we keep, and they give charity out of their surplus riches. Upon this he (the Holy Prophet {may peace and blessing be upon him}) said: Has not prescribed for you a course by which you can also do charity? In every declaration of the glorification of Allah (i.e. saying Subhan Allah) there is a charity. In every praise of His (saying al-hamdu lillah) is a Charity. In every declaration that He is One (La ilaha ill Allah) is a charity. Enjoining of good is a charity. In every forbidding of what is evil is a charity, and in a man's sexual inercourse with his wife there is a charity. They (the companions) said: Do you see, if he were to devote it to something forbidden, would it not be a sin on his part? Similarly if he were to devote it to something lawful, he should have a reward for it.

Sahih Muslim

Book #2 p.108, #1006

Umar ibn Al-Khattab (*RadyiAllahu Anhu*) reported: The Messenger of Allah (may peace and blessing be upon him) ordered us to give Charity and at the time I possessed some wealth. I said to myself, "Today I will outdo Abu Bakr (*RadyiAllahu Anhu*), if ever there were a day to outdo him". I went with half of my wealth to the Prophet and he said, "What have you left for your family? I said, " The same amount." Then Abu Bakr (*RadyiAllahu Anhu*) came with everything he had. The Prophet said, "O Abu Bakr (*RadyiAllahu Anhu*), What have you left for your family?" Abu Bakr (*RadyiAllahu Anhu*) said "Allah and his Messenger'. I said, "By Allah, I will never do better than Abu Bakr (*RadyiAllahu Anhu*)".

Sunan Al- Tirmidhi 3675

Graded Sahih (Authentic)

The Prophet (may peace and blessing be upon him) said: When a person dies, all his deeds come to an end except three: Sadaqa Jaariyah (ongoing charity), beneficial knowledge (which he has left behind) or a righteous child who will pray for him"

Al-Tirmidhi #1376

Sahih Hasan

Zakat Al- Fitr is obligatory for every Muslim at the end of Ramadan as a expiation for any mistakes he or she committed during this month. This charity must be paid before the Eid prayer in a very specific amount.

Narrated Ibn Umar (*RadyiAllahu Anhu*): Allah's Messenger (may peace and blessing be upon him) made it the payment of one Sa of Dates or one Sa of barley as Zak12at-ul Fitr on every muslim slave or free, male or female, young or old; and he ordered that it be paid before the people went out to offer Eid. (one Sa= 3 Kilograms approx.)

Sahih Al Bukhari

Book#2 p.338, #1503

Abu Huraira (*RadyiAllahu Anhu*) reported that Allah's Messenger (may peace and blessing be upon him) has said: Charity does not in any way decrease the wealth of the servant who pardons, Allah adds to his respect, and the one who shows humility, Allah elevated him in the estimation of the people.

Sahih Muslim #2588

Allah said in Surah 102 At Takathur 8. **Then on that Day you shall be asked about the delights you indulged in, in this world!**

Narrated Abu Hurairah (*RadyiAllahu Anhu*): Once during a day or a night Allah's Messenger (may peace and blessing be upon him) came out and found Abu Bakr (*RadyiAllahu Anhu*) and Umar (*RadyiAllahu Anhu*) he said: What brings you out of your homes at this hour? They replied, "Hunger, O Allah's Messenger". He said: By Him (Allah) in whose Hand my soul is, I too have come out for the same reason for which you have come out". Then He (may peace and blessing be upon him) said to both of them: Come along! And he went along with them to a man from the Ansar, but they did not find him in his house. The wife of the man saw the prophet (may peace and blessing be upon him) and said: " You are welcome". Allah's Messenger (may peace and blessing be upon him) asked her (saying): where is so-and-so? " She replied: He has gone to fetch some water for us. In the meantime the Ansari man came, saw Allah's Messenger (may peace and blessing be upon him) with his two companions and said: "All praise and thanks be to Allah: Today there is none superior to me as regards guests. Then he went and brought a part of a bunch of dates- Fruit, having dates, some still green, some ripe and some fully ripe and requested them to eat from it. He then took his knife (to slaughter a sheep for them). Allah's Messenger (may peace and blessing be upon him) said to him Beware! Do not slaughter a milch sheep". So he slaughtered a sheep (prepared the meals from its meat). They ate from that sheep and that bunch of dates and drank water. After they had finished eating and drinking to their full, Allah's Messenger (may peace and blessing be upon him) said to Abu Bakr (*RadyiAllahu Anhu*) and Umar (*RadyiAllahu Anhu*): By him in whose hand is my soul is, you will be asked about this treat on the Day of Resurrection. He (Allah) brought you out of your homes with hunger and you are not returning to your homes till you have been blessed with this treat".

Sahih Muslim
Vol 6 The Book of Drink
Charter 20 p. 116, 117

Having wealth is a delight of this life and in this hadith we see that Allah will ask us about every delight even a meal which is a treat. Sharing our wealth is an act of worship, whether its obligatory charity or the volunteer and Allah accepts our good deeds if our intentions are pure.

It was narrated from Abu Hurayrah (may Allah be pleased with him) that the Messenger of Allah (blessings and peace of Allah be upon him) said: "A man said: I shall certainly give charity. He went out with his charity and placed it in the hand of a thief. The next morning, they said: He gave charity to a thief. He said: O Allah, praise be to You; I shall certainly give charity (again). He went out with his charity and placed it in the hands of a prostitute. The next morning they said: Last night he gave charity to a prostitute. He said: O Allah, praise be to You for a prostitute. I shall certainly give charity (again).' He went out with his charity and placed it in the hand of a rich man. The next morning, they said, Last night he gave charity to a rich man. He said: O Allah, to You be praise for a thief, a prostitute and a rich man. It was said to him: As for what you gave in charity to a thief, perhaps it will be the cause of his refraining from stealing; as for the prostitute, perhaps it will be the cause of her refraining from fornication; and as for the rich man, perhaps he will learn a lesson and spend from that which Allah has given him."

Narrated by al-Bukhaari, 1355; Muslim, 1022

Ramadan

Allah Said in Surah 2 Al-Baqarah 185. **The Month of Ramathan in which was revealed the Qur'an a guidance for Mankind and clear proofs from the guidance and the criterion between right and wrong, So whoever sights the crescent on the first night of the month of Ramathan, He must observe Saum (Fast) that month, and whoever is ill or on a journey, the same number[of days which one did not observe Saum (Fast) must be made up] from other days. Allah intends for you ease, and He does not want to make things difficult for you. He wants that you must complete the same number of days, and that you must magnify Allah [i.e. to say Takbir- Allahu Abar; Allah is the Most Great)] for having guided you so that you may be grateful to him.**

Allah praised the month of Ramathan out of the other months by choosing it to send down the Glorious Quran, just as He did for all the Divine books he revealed to the prophets.

Imam Ahmad reported Wathilah bin Al-Asqu that Allah's Messenger (may peace and blessing be upon him) said: The sufuf (Pages) of Ibrahim (AS) were revealed during the first night of Ramathan. The Torah was revealed during the first night of Ramathan. The Injil was revealed during the thirteenth night of Ramathan. Allah revealed the Qur'an on the twenty-fourth night of Ramathan.

Ahmad 4:107

Allah said in Surah 97 Al Qadr 1. **Verily we have sent it (this Qur'an) down in the night of Al- Qadr (Decree).**

Allah said in Surah 44 Ad-Dukhan 1. **Ha Mim 2. By the manifest Book (the Qur'an) that makes things clear. 3. We sent it (the Qur'an) down on a blessed night [(i.e. the night of Al-Qadr)]. Verily we are ever warning mankind that our Torment will reach those who disbelieve in the oneness of Lordship and in our oneness of worship.**

The view of the majority is that the Qur'an was sent down from Al-Lawh Al Manfooz (The Preserved Tablet) to the first heaven on Laylat-al Qadr (the night of Decree) all at once, then after that it was sent down in stages of twenty-three years

Allah said in Surah 85 Al-Burooj 21. **Nay! This is a Glorious Quran 22. Inscribed in Al- Lauh Al-Mahfuz (The preserved Tablets)!**

Allah said in Surah 25 Al- Furqan 32. **And those who disbelieve say: "Why is not the Qur'an revealed to him all at once?" Thus it is sent down in parts, that we may strengthen your heart thereby. And we have revealed it to you gradually, in stages (it was revealed to the Prophet (may peace and blessings be upon him) in 23 years).**

Allah said in Surah 18 Al Kahf 106. **And it is a Qur'an which we have divided into parts, in order that you might recite it to men at intervals, And we have revealed it by stages in 23 years.**

It was narrated That Ibn Abbas (*RadyiAllahu Anhu*) said concerning the verse "Verily! We have sent it (this Qur'an) down in the night of Al-Qadr (Decree)." The Qur'an was sent all at once on Layla til-Qadr, then Allah sent it down to the Messenger of Allah (may peace and blessing be upon him) bit-by-bit. "And those who disbelieve say: Why is not the Qur'an revealed to him all at once? Thus it is sent down in parts, that we may strengthen your heart thereby. We have revealed it to you gradually in stages (25:32)

An Nasaa'i

Allah started the revelation

Narrated Aisha (*RadyiAllahu Anha*) the mother of the faithful believers: The commencement of the Divine Revelation to Allah's Messenger (may peace and blessing be upon him) was in the form of good righteous (true) dreams which came true like bright daylight, and then the love of seclusion in the Cave of Hira where he used to worship (Allah alone) continuously for many nights before returning to (or he desire to see) his family. He used to take with him the journey food for the stay and then come back to his wife Khadijah to take his food likewise again till suddenly the Truth descended upon him while he was in the Cave of Hira. The Angel came to him and asked him to Read, The Prophet (may peace and blessing be upon him) replied, "I do not know how to read."

The Prophet (may peace and blessing be upon him) added, then the Angel caught me forcefully and pressed me so hard that I could not bear it anymore. He then released me and again asked me to read and I replied, I do not know how to read. There upon he caught me again and pressed me a second time till I could not bear it any more. He then released me and again asked me to read but again I replied, I do not know how to read (or what shall I read?) Thereupon he caught me for the third time and pressed me, and then released and said 'Read in the name of your Lord, Who created all that exists. Has created man from a clot a piece of thick coagulated blood. Read! And your Lord is Most Generous." Surah 96:1-3

Sahih Al Bukhari

Book #1 p. 46 #3

It is not a new or strange concept that Angel Gabriel comes to a prophet calling him to know his mission. As a Matter of fact we believe that Angel Gabriel went to All the prophets and we can find this exact interaction in Daniel 9:20-23. 20 While I was speaking and praying, confessing my sin and the sin of my people Israel and making my request to the Lord my God for his holy hill— 21 while I was still in prayer, Gabriel, the man I had seen in the earlier vision, came to me in swift flight about the time of the evening sacrifice. 22 He instructed me and said to me, "Daniel, I have now come to give you insight and understanding. 23 As soon as you began to pray, a word went out, which I have come to tell you, for you are highly esteemed. Therefore, consider the word and understand the vision:

We should all know that the Isnad of the Seerah in the Books of History does not always reach the level of Sahih however in Allah's word (the best of speech is the speech of Allah {the Book of Allah-The Qur'an}) the verses are preserved for us all to see, for example the accusation that was made against the Prophet's (may peace and blessing be upon him) wife (RA) is found in the book of Allah where

Allah said in Surah 24 AnNur 11 **Verily, those who brought forth the slander against Aishah (RA) the wife of the Prophet (may peace and blessing be upon him) are a group among you.**

And

When the Uncle of the Prophet (may peace and blessing be upon him) Abu Lahab rebuked him harshly.

Narrated Ibn Abbas (*RadyiAllahu Anhu*): When the verse, 'And warn your tribe O Muhammad (may peace and blessing be upon him) of near kindred (V26 Ash-Shu'ara 214) was revealed, Allah's Messenger (may peace and blessing be upon him)went out, and when he had ascended

As-Safa Mountain, he shouted, Ya Sahabah! The people said, 'What is that?' Then they gathered around him, whereupon he said. 'Do you see? If I inform you that cavalryman and proceeding up the side of this mountain, will you believe me?' They said, 'We have never heard you telling a lie.' Then he said, 'I am a plain warner to you of a coming severe punishment.' Abu Lahab said, May you perish! You gathered us only for this reason?' Then Abu Lahab went away. So Surat Al- Masad' **Perish the hands of Abu Lahab!** Was revealed (V111:1)

Sahih Al Bukhari

Book 6 # 495

We too must find the solutions to our life situation in the Qur'an and Hadith. In the month of Ramadan we should refresh our relationship with the Qur'an. One of the miracles of the Qur'an is that every time you read it you find something else new that you never saw before as Allah takes the veil off our ears, eyes, and heart. As for example, when our beloved Prophet (may peace and blessing be upon him) passed away Umar became overwhelmed by his emotions and distressed by the companions saying that the Messenger of Allah (may peace and blessing be upon him) passed away. Umar (RA) said if anyone else says that the Messenger of Allah (may peace and blessing be upon him) passed away, he will hit his neck with my sword. Then Abu Bakr (RadyiAllahu Anhu) came addressed the people by reciting the verse from Surah 3 Al-Imran Ayat 144 **Muhammad is no more than a Messenger, and Messengers have passed away before him. If, then, he were to die or be slain will you turn about on your heels? Whoever turns about on his heels can in no way harm Allah. As for the grateful ones, Allah will soon reward them.** *Umar (RA) said that it was as if this was the first time he ever heard this verse and this is a phenomenon of the Qur'an which we all experience and our relationship with the Qur'an brings extreme joy.*

Narrated Ibn Abbas (*RadyiAllahu Anhu*): The Prophet (may peace and blessing be upon him) was the most generous amongst the people, and he used to be more so in the month of Ramadan when Jibril (Gabriel) visited him, and Jibril used to meet him on every night of Ramadan till the end of the month. The Prophet (may peace and blessing be upon him) used to recite the Noble Qur'an to Jibril, and when Jibril met him, he used to be more generous than the fair wind sent by Allah with glad tidings (rain) in readiness and haste to do charitable deeds

Sahih Al Bukhari

Book 3 p.83, #1902

Allah had supported the Prophets with various miracles and signs to confirm the truth of their Prophethood. For example, in the case of Moses (may peace and blessing be upon him), his staff turned into a fast moving snake, the Sea was parted for him, and he put his hand into his garment and it became completely white. Allah, may he be Glorified and Exalted, said to him in

Surah 28 Al-Qasas 31. **And throw your stick!" But when he saw it moving as if it were a snake, he turned in flight, and looked not back. It was said: "O Musa (Moses)! Draw near, and fear not. Verily, you are of those who are secure. 32.**

"Put your hand in your bosom, it will come forth white without a disease; and draw your hand close to your side to be free from the fear (which you suffered from the snake, and also your hand will return to its original state). These are two Burhan (signs, miracles, evidences, proofs) from your Lord to Fir'aun (Pharaoh) and his Chiefs. Verily, they are the people who are fasiqun (rebellious, disobedient to Allah).

Isa (Jesus {may peace and blessing be upon him}) spoke in the cradle as an infant, and he used to heal those who had been born blind and lepers, and raise the dead by Allah's leave, and a table from heaven was sent down to him for his people.

Allah said in Surah 5 Al- Ma'idah 110. **(Remember) when Allah will say (on the Day of Resurrection). "O Isa (Jesus), son of Maryam (Mary)! Remember My Favour to you and your mother when I supported you with *Ruh-ul-Qudus* [Jibrael (Gabriel)] so that you spoke to the people in the cradle and in maturity; and when I taught you writing, Al-Hikmah (the power of understanding), the Taurat (Torah) and the Injeel Gospel); and when you made out of the clay, a figure like that of a bird, by My Permission, and you breathed into it, and it become a bird by My Permission, and you healed those born blind, and the lepers by My Permission, and when you brought forth the dead by My Permission: and when I restrained the Children of Israel from you (when they resolve to kill you) as you came unto them with clear proofs, and the disbelievers among them said: 'This is nothing but evident magic.'"**

It is Narrated on the Authority of Abu Huraira (RA) that the Messenger of Allah (may peace and blessing be upon him) said: There has never been a Prophet of the Prophets who was not bestowed with a sign amongst the signs which were bestowed (on the earlier prophets). Human beings believed in it and verily I have been conferred upon revelation (the Holy Qur'an) which Allah revealed to me. I hope that I will have the greatest followers on the Day of Resurrection.

Sahih Muslim
Book 1 p. 127, #152

Abd Allah B. Amr reported the Apostle of Allah (may peace and blessing be upon him) as saying: One who was devoted to the Qur'an will be told to recite, ascend and recite carefully as he recited carefully when he was in the world, for he will reach his abode when he comes to the last verse he recites.

Sunan Abu Dawud
Book #1 p. 384, #1459

Abu Huraira (*RadyiAllahu Anhu*) reported that Allah's Messenger (may peace and blessing be upon him) said: Allah the Exalted and Majestic said: Every act of the son of Adam (AS) is for him, except fasting. It is exclusively meant for me and I alone will reward it. Fasting is a shield. When any of you fasts a day, he should neither indulge in obscene language, nor raise the voice. If anyone reviles him or tries to quarrel with him he should say: I am a fasting person. By Him in Whose Hand is the life of Muhammad, the breath of that one who fast is sweeter to Allah, on the Day of Judgement, than the fragrance of Musk. The one who fast has two occasions of joy, one when he breaks the fasts, he is glad with the breaking of the fast and one when he meets his Lord, he is glad with his fast.

Sahih Muslim

Book 2 p.192 #1151

Celebrating the Guidance

When Allah created Adam (AS) Allah kept him in Nearness to him by allowing him to live in Paradise and gave him an open reign throughout the Garden except from one Tree. Allah fashioned Adam with His own Hand and taught him the name of all things. Allah defended the honor of Adam from the accusation of the Angels and made them bow down to him in obedience to Allah. Allah created a Wife from the Rib of Adam to support him with some companionship and One of the greatest honors Adam had was that Allah spoke directly to him. Despite all of these advantages (Love) it was the Kuddar that Adam would be influenced by the waswasa (whispering, suggestions) of the Shaytan. Of All the Trees in the Paradise the shaytan made the one Tree that Allah told Adam to stay away from seem Alluring. Allah made Adam, Eve (Hawwa) and Shaytan slip from the Paradise to go down to the Earth as a result of his disobedience. Adam's repentance was accepted

64

but the consequence of his action was to live on Earth for a time but Allah gave Adam words of inspiration.

Allah said in Surah 2 Al Baqarah 38. **We Said: "Get down all of you from this place (the Paradise), then wherever there comes to you Guidance from me, and whoever follows My Guidance, there Shall be no fear on them, nor shall they grieve.**

This Quran is the Guidance as

Allah said in Surah Al-Baqarah 1. **Alif Lam Mim 2. This is the Book (the Qur'an), whereof there is no doubt, a guidance to those who are Al Muttaqun (Pious).**

Allah also said in Surah 3 Ali Imran 7. **It is He who has sent down to you {Muhammad (may peace and blessing be upon him)} the Book (this Qur'an). In it are verses that are entirely clear, they are the foundations of the Book; and others not entirely clear. So as for those in whose hearts there is a deviation from the truth they follow that which is not which is not entirely clear thereof, Seeking Al- Fitnah, and seeking for its hidden meanings, but none knows its hidden meaning save Allah. And those who are firmly grounded in Knowledge Say:" We believe in it;the whole of it (clear and unclear) verses are from our Lord". And none receive admonition except men of understanding.**

The Month of Ramadan is the celebration of Allah's promise to Adam that he would send him Guidance as

Allah said in Surah 2 Al Baqarah 185. **The Month of Ramadan in which was revealed the Qur'an, a guidance and the criterion between right and wrong. So whosoever of you sights the crescent on the first night of the month, he must observe Saum (Fasts) that month, and whoever is ill or on a journey, the same number of days must be made** up from other days. Allah intends for you ease, and He doesn't want to make things difficult for you. He wants that you must complete the same number of Days and that you must Magnify Allah for having guided you so that you may be grateful to Him.

Narrated Mu'awiya (*RadyiAllahu Anhu*) in a khutbah (religious talk): I heard Allah's Messenger (may peace and blessing be upon him) saying, "If Allah wants to do good to a person, He makes him comprehend the religion [the understanding of the Qur'an and As-Sunna (Legal ways) of the Prophet Muhammad (may peace and blessing be upon him)]. I am just a distributor, but the grant is Allah (azawajal) and remember that this nation (true muslims- real followers of Islamic Monotheism) will remain obedient to Allah's Orders [i.e. Following strictly Allah's Book (the Qur;an) and the Prophet's Sunnah (legal ways)] and they will not be harmed by anyone who will oppose them (going on a different path), till Allah's Order (Day of Judgement) is established".

Sahih Al-Bukhari
P.98 Book 1 #71

Love is defined as an intense feeling of deep affection

Habbun حب *which means to Love, Like, Wish*

The root word and its 19 different forms has been used in the Qur'an 83 times.

Allah spoke about Mankind's Love of things in 13 Surahs like where he said in

Surah 14 Ibrahim 3. **Those who Love the life of this world to the hereafter, and hinder men from the path of Allah (i.e. Islam) and seek crookedness therein -- They are far astray.**

And

Allah 3 Ali Imran 14. **Beautified for men is the Love of things they covet; women, children, much of gold and silver (wealth), branded beautiful horses, cattle and well-tilled land. This is the pleasure of the present world's life; but Allah has the excellent return (Paradise) with flowing rivers with Him.**

Of course everyone defines Love specific to themselves and those who think they are showing Love is not always received as such. For instance, a wife says my Husband doesn't Love me because he never says I Love you Baby. However the Husband says my wife knows I love her because I pay all the bills and take good care of her. Even though both have evidence of their Love but if the specific checklist is not met the Love seems void.

Wa lillahi wa mathalul Alla (and to Allah is the best example)

Allah said in Surah 2 Al Baqarah 165. **And of mankind are some who take (for worship) other besides Allah as rivals to Allah. They Love them as they Love Allah. But those who believe, love Allah more than anything else. If only, those who do wrong could see, when they will see the torment, that all power belongs to Allah and that Allah is Severe in Punishment.**

Allah said in Surah 9 At Taubah 24. **Say: If your fathers, your sons, your brothers, your wives, your kindred, the wealth that you have gained, the commerce in which you fear a decline, and the dwellings in which you delight are dearer to you than Allah and His Messenger, and striving hard and fighting in his cause then wait until Allah brings about his Decision (torment). And Allah guides not the people who are Al Fasiqun (rebellious, disobedient to Allah).**

Allah tells how he wants to be Loved in

Surah 3 Ali Imran 31. **Say (O Muhammad [may peace and blessing be upon him]) to mankind "If you really Love Allah then follow me, Allah will love you and Forgive you of your sins. And Allah is Oft Forgiving, Most Merciful".**

Narrated Abu Hurairah (*RadyiAllahu Anhu*): Allah's Messenger (may peace and blessing be upon him) said, "Allah said, 'I will declare war against him who shows hostility to a pious worshipper of mine. And the most beloved things with which My slave comes nearer to me, is what I have enjoined upon him; and my slaves keeps on coming closer to Me through performing Nawafil (Prayers or doing extra deeds beside what is obligatory) till I Love him, then I become his sense of hearing with which he hears, and his sense of sight with which he sees, and his hand which he grips, and his legs with which he walks; and if he ask me, I will give him, and if he asks my protection (Refuge), I will protect him (i.e. give him My refuge); and I do not hesitate to do anything Like I do to take the soul of the believer, for he hates death, and I hate to disappoint him".

Sahih Al Bukhari
Book 8, p. 275 #6502

Narrated Abu Hurairah (*RadyiAllahu Anhu*): Allah's Messenger (may peace and blessing be upon him) said," If Allah (Tabarak Watallah) Loves a person, He calls Jabril (Gabriel), saying 'Allah loves so-and-so, So Jabril would make an announcement in the heavens: "Allah has loved so-and-so therefore you should love him also. So all the dwellers of the heavens would love him, and then he is granted the pleasure of the people on the earth."

Sahih Al Bukhari8
Book 9 p. 251, #7485

The Story of how the first Jinn of this Ummah became Muslim was narrated by Abd-Allah ibn Abbas (RA), who said: "The Prophet (may peace and blessing be upon him) went out with a group of his Companions heading for the marketplace of Ukaaz. This was when the shayteen were prevented from getting any news from heaven and shooting stars had been sent against them. The Shayteen went back to their people, who said, "what is the matter with you?" They said, "We cannot get news from heaven, and shooting stars were sent against us." Their people said, "nothing is stopping you from hearing new from heaven." Those who went out in the direction of Tihaamah came upon The Prophet (may peace and blessing be upon him) in Nakhlah, when he was leading his companions in Fajr prayer. When they heard the Qur'an, they listened to it and said, "By Allah, this is what is stopping us from hearing the news from heaven". When they went back to the people they said, "O our people, we have heard a wonderful recital (The Qur'an). It guides to the Right Path, and we have believed therein, and we shall never join in worship any with our Lord (Allah). [Al Jinn 72:] Then Allah revealed to me that a group of Jinn listened to theis Quran [Al Jinn 72:1], and Allah revealed to him what the Jinn had said."

Sahih Al Bukhari 731

Narrated Abu Hurairah (RA):Allah's Messenger (may peace and blessing be upon him) said, "When the Month of Ramadan starts, the gates of heaven are opened and the gates of Hell are closed and the devils are chained."

Sahih Al Bukhari
Vol 3, p. 82, #1899

"This is the month of Ramadan in which was Revealed the Qur'an, and a guidance for mankind and clear proof and a criterion between right and wrong". So in this Month we will get a much better result at calling mankind by the Qur'an. So every Ramathan we notice a phenomenon where the masjids

are full, Muslims are visibly striving, and the ones who don't practiced their religion throughout the year, their faith increases to its full potential.

Gratitude For Allah

Allah tells us the purpose of Life as we strive to be the Best worshippers we can be in the Blessed month of Ramathan. At the end of this Ayat Allah said

Surah 2 Al Baqarah 185. **Allah intends for you ease, and He does not want to make things difficult for you. He wants that you must complete the same number of days, and that you must magnify Allah for having guided you so that you may be grateful to Him.**

Allah said in Surah 16 An Nahl 18. **And if you would count the favours of Allah, never could you be able to count them. Truly, Allah is Oft-Forgiving, Most Merciful.**

So Allah want us to be grateful and the Shaytan want you to be ungrateful

Surah 7 Al-A'raf 17. **Then I will come to them from before them and behind them, from their right and from their left, and you will not find most of them as thankful ones (i.e. You will not find them dutiful to you).**

As Muslims, the holidays we celebrate is Jummah (Friday) service, and the two Eids (Eid Al Adha and Eid Al Fitr) but as we get close to end of the Month of Ramathan we prepare to have a feast, but we must realize the Shaytan is about to be released.

Narrated Abu Hurayrah (RA) that the Messenger of Allah (may peace and blessing be upon him) said: "When Ramathan comes, the gates of Paradise are opened, the gates of Hell are closed, and the devils are chained up".

Al-Bukhaari (1899) and Muslim (1079)

Shukr Allah(Thanking Allah) & Alhumd iLLah (Praising Allah) are tools we use against Shayton as well as all the habits we have become used to during this month of Ramathan. In the month of Ramathan our acts of ibadah (worship) lock the Shaytan up. Our Fasting, reading the Quran, Taraweeh (Night Prayer) in congregation, Sadaqa (charity), Those who sponsor Iftar (Meals for breaking the fast), etc. make the works of shaytan useless. Iman (Belief\ Faith) implies being Thankful and Grateful and the opposite is Kufr (disbelief) or ungratefulness.

Allah said in Surah2 Al Baqarah 152. **Therefore remember Me (by Praying and glorifying). I will remember you, and be grateful to me for my countless favour on you and never be ungrateful to me.**

Narrated Abu Hurairah (RA): The Prophet (may peace and blessings be upon him) said: Allah (Azzawajjal), says, I am just as My Slave thinks I am, and I am with him if he remembers Me. If he remembers Me in himself, I too, remember him in Myself; and if he remembers Me in a group of people, I remember him in a group that is better than them; and if he comes one span nearer to me, I go one cubit nearer to him; and if he comes one cubit nearer to me, I go a distance of two outstretched arms nearer to him; and if he comes to me walking, I go to him running."

Sahih Al Bukhari Vol. 9 #502

Being Grateful to Allah is the Sunnah (Legal way) of all the Prophets as Allah tells about Ibrahim in

Surah 16 AnNahl 120. **Verily, Ibrahim (Abraham) was an Ummah (a leader having all the good righteous qualities) or a nation, obedient to Allah, Hanifa (i.e. to worship none but Allah), and he was not one of those who are Al- Mushrikun (polytheists, idolaters, disbelievers**

in the Oneness of Allah, and those who joined partners with Allah).
121. He was thankful for His (Allah's) favours. He (Allah) chose
him as an intimate friend and guided him to a Straight Path (Islamic
Monotheism - neither Judaism nor Christianity).

Allah told us about Noah in

Surah 17 Al- Isra 3. **"O offspring of those whom we carried in the
Ship with Nuh (Noah)! Verily, he was a grateful slave".**

*As for Abu Qasim {Prophet Muhammad (may peace and blessing be
upon him)}*

Aisha (RA) reported that when Allah's Messenger (may peace and
blessing be upon him) occupied himself in prayer, he observed a long
posture of standing in prayer that his feet were swollen. A'isha said:
Allah's Messenger (may peace and blessing be upon him), you do this in
spite of the fact that your earlier and later sin have been pardoned not I
prove myself to be a thankful servant of Allah?

Sahih Muslim
Book #4 #2821

Being grateful to Allah is for you

Allah tells us through his inspiration to Luqman in Surah 31
Luqman 12

**And indeed we bestowed upon Luqman Al-Hikmah (Wisdom)
saying: Give thanks to Allah." And whoever gives thanks, he gives
thanks for the good of his ownself and whoever is unthankful, then
verily, Allah is All- Rich (free of all needs, worthy of all praise).**

We must be grateful for every morsel of food and Fasting teaches us that.

Allah said in Surah2 Al Baqarah 172. **O you who believe (in the Oneness of Allah-Islamic Monotheism)! Eat of the lawful things that We have provided you with, and be grateful to Allah, if it is indeed He whom you worship.**

Abu Huraira (RA) reported that Allah's Messenger (may peace and blessing be upon him) went out of his house one day or one night, and there he found Abu Bakr (RA) and Umar (RA) also. He said: What has brought you out of your houses at this hour? They said: Allah's Messenger (may peace and blessing be upon him), it is hunger. Thereupon he said: By him in whose hand is my life, what has brought you out has brought me out too; Get up. They got up along with him, and all of them came to the house of an Ansari, but he was not home. When his wife saw him (may peace and blessing be upon him), she said: Most welcome, and Allah's Messenger (may peace and blessing be upon him) said to her: Where is so and so? She said: He has gone to get some fresh water for us. When the Ansari came and he saw Allah's Messenger (may peace and blessing be upon him) and his two companions, he said: Praise be to Allah, no one has more honourable guests today than I have. He then went out and brought them a bunch of ripe dates, dry dates and fresh dates, and said: Eat some of them. He then took hold of his long knife (for slaughtering a goat or a sheep). Allah's Messenger (may peace and blessing be upon him) said to him: Beware of killing a milch animal. He slaughtered a sheep for them and after they had eaten of it and of the bunch of date and drank, and when they had taken their fill and had been fully satisfied with the drink, Allah's Messenger (may peace and blessing be upon him) said to Abu Bakr and Umar: By Him in whose Hand is my Life, you will certainly be questioned about this bounty on the Day of Judgement. Hunger brought you out of your house, then you didn't return until this bounty came to you.

Sahih Muslim
Book #3 p.382, #2038

Ramathan replenishes our gratitude for the favours Allah bestows upon us.

Abu Hurayrah (RA) said: The Messenger of Allah (may peace and blessing be upon him) said: Every deed of the sons of Adam will be multiplied between ten and seven hundred times. Allah (Highly exalted is he) said except fasting. It is for Me and I shall reward for it. He gives up his desires and his food for my sake."

Narrated by Muslim 1151

Sahl (RA) said that the Prophet (may peace and blessings be upon him) said: "In Paradise there is a gate called Al- Rayyan, through which those who used to fast will enter on the day of Resurrection, and no one but they will enter it. It will be said, "Where are those who fasted? They will get up and none will enter it but them. When they have entered, it will be locked, and no one else will enter.

Al Bukhari 1763
Muslim 1947

It was narrated from Abu Salaamah that Abu Hurayrah (RA) said: The Messenger of Allah (may peace and blessings be upon him) said: Whoever fasts Ramadan out of faith and seeking reward, his previous sins will be forgiven."

Narrated by Al Bukhari
Book of Iman #37

Abu Ayyoob (RA) reported that the Messenger of Allah (may peace and blessing be upon him) said: "Whoever fasts Ramadan and follows it with six days of Shawwal, it will be as if he fasted for a lifetime."

Narrated by Muslim, Abu Dawud, Al Tirmidhi, Al-Nisa, and Ibn Majah

If we look at one of the slaves of Allah who was granted many gifts we notice his gratitude which is the ways of the believers. Allah tells us about the gifts of Sulaiman (AS)

Surah 38 Sad 35. **He said: My Lord! Forgive me, and bestow upon me a kingdom such as shall not belong to any other after me: Verily, You are the bestower." 36. So, We subjected to him the winds; it blew gently by his order wither so ever he willed. 37. And also the Shayatin (devils) from the Jinn (including) every king of builder and diver. 38. And also others bound in fetters. 39. Allah said to Sulaiman (Soloman): This is our gift: So spend you or withhold, no account will be asked of you.**

Allah said in Surah 34 Saba 12. **And to Solomon we subjected the wind, it's morning (stride from sunrise till midnoon) was a month's journey, and it's afternoon (stride from the midday decline of the sun to sunset) was a month's journey). And we caused a fount of (molten) brass to flow from him, and there was Jinn that worked in front of him, by the leave of his Lord. And whosoever of them turned aside from Our command, We shall cause him to taste of the torment of the blazing fire. 12. They worked for him as he desired, (making) high rooms, images, basins as large as reservoirs, and (cooking) cauldrons fixed in their places).**

Allah said in Surah 27. AnNaml 19. **So he [Sulaiman (Solomon)] smiled, amused at her speech and said: My Lord! Inspire me and** bestow upon me the power and ability that I may be grateful for Your Favours which you have bestowed on me and on my parents, and that I may do righteous good deeds that will please You, and admit me by Your Mercy among Your righteous slaves."

Gratitude to Allah is the purpose of life as

Allah said in Surah 102 At Takathus 8 **Then on that Day you shall be asked about the delights (you indulged in, in this world)!**

Hajj

The Hajj (pilgrimage) is an annual Islamic Pilgrimage to Mecca, which is the holiest city in the world. Hajj is a mandatory religious duty which must be done at least once in their lifetime by all muslims who are physically and financially capable of unterking the journey, and can support their family during their absence. The rites of Hajj, which go back to Prophet Abraham.

Allah said in Surah 2 Al-Baqarah 125. **And (remember) when We made the House (the Ka'bah at Makkah) a place of resort for mankind and a place of safety. And take you (people) the Maqam (Place) of Ibrahim (Abraham [or the stone on which Ibrahim (Abraham {AS} stood while he was building the ka'bah at Makkah), and we commanded Ibrahim (Abraham) and Isma'il (Ishmael) that they should purify My House (the Ka'bah at Makkah) for those who are circumambulating it, or staying (I'tikaf), or bowing or prostrating themself (there, in prayer). 126. And (remember) when Ibrahim (Abraham) said, "My Lord, make this city (Makkah) a place of security and provide its people with fruits, such of them as believe in Allah and the Last Day." He (Allah) answered: "As for him who disbelieves, I shall leave him in contentment for a while, then I shall compel him to the torment of the Fire, and worst indeed is that destination!" 127. And (Remember) when Ibrahim (Abraham) and** (his son) Isma'il (Ishmael) were raising the foundations of the House (the Ka'bah at Makkah), (saying), "Our Lord! Accept (this service) from us. Verily! You are the All-Hearer, the All-Knower."

Allah said in Surah 22. Al-Hajj 26. And (Remember) when we showed Ibrahim (Abraham) the site of the (Sacred) House (The Ka'bah at Makkah) (saying): "Associate not anything (in worship) with Me, [La ilaha illallah (none has the right to be worshipped with Allah)-- Islamic Monotheism], and sanctify My House for those who circumambulate it, and those stand up (for prayer), and those who bow (submit themselves with humility and obedience to Allah), and make prostration (in prayer);" 27. And proclaim to mankind to Hajj (pilgrimage). They will come to you on foot and on every lean camel, they will come from every deep and distant (wide) mountain highway (to perform Hajj). 28. That they may witness things that are of benefit to them (i.e. reward of Hajj in the Hereafter, and also some worldly gain from trade), and mention the Name of Allah on appointed days (i.e. 10th, 11th, 12th, and 13th day of Dhul-Hijjah), over the beast of cattle that He has provided for them (for sacrifice), [at the time of their slaughtering by saying: (Bismillah, Wallahu- Akbar, Allahumma Minka wa Ilaik)]. Then eat thereof and feed therewith the poor who have a very hard time. 29. Then let them complete their prescribed duties (Manasik of Hajj) and perform their vows, and circumambulate the Ancient House (the Ka'bah at Makkah). 30. That (Manasik -- prescribed duties of Hajj is the obligation that mankind owes to Allah) and whoever honours the sacred things of Allah, then that is better for him with his Lord. The cattle are lawful to you, except those (that will be) mentioned to you (as exceptions) So shun the abomination (worshipping) of idols, and shun lying speech (False statements) 31. Hunafa Lillah (i.e. worshiping none but Allah), not associating partners (in worship) unto Him; and whoever assigns partners to Allah, it is as if he had fallen from the sky, and the birds had snatched him, or the wind had thrown him to a far off place. 32. Thus it is [what has been mentioned in the above said Verses (27, 28, 29, 30, 31) is an obligation that mankind owes to Allah] and whosoever honours the Symbols of Allah, then it is truly, from the piety of the hearts. 33. In them (cattle offered for sacrifice) are benefits for you for an appointed term, and afterwards they are brought for sacrifice unto the ancient House (the Haram-- sacred territory of Makkah). 34. And for every nation We have appointed religious ceremonies, that they may mention the Name of Allah over the beast of cattle that He has given them for food, And your Ilah (God) is One Ilah (God --Allah), so you must submit to Him Alone (in Islam), And {O Muhammad (may peace and blessing be upon him)} give glad tidings to the Mukhbitum [those who obey Allah with humility and are humble from among the true believers of Islamic Monotheism],

Ja'far b Muhammad reported on the authority of his father: We went to Jabir b. Abdullah and he began inquiring about the people (who had gone to see him) till it was my turn. I said: I am Muhammad b. 'Ali b. Husain. He placed his hand upon my head and opened my upper button and then the lower one and then placed his palm on my chest (in order to bless me), and I was, during those days, a young boy, and he said: You are welcome, my nephew. Ask whatever you want to ask. And I asked him but as he was blind (he could not respond to me immediately), and the time for prayer came. He stood up covering himself in his mantle. And whenever he placed its ends upon his shoulders they slipped down on account of being short (in size). Another mantle was, however, lying on the clothes rack nearby. And he led us in the prayer. I said to him: Tell me about the Hajj of Allah's Messenger (May peace be upon him).

And he pointed with his hand nine, and then stated: The Messenger of Allah (may peace be upon him) stayed in (Medina) for nine years but did not perform Hajj, then he made a public announcement in the tenth year to the effect that Allah's Messenger (may peace be upon him) was about to perform the Hajj. A large number of persons came to Medina and all of them were anxious to follow the Messenger of Allah (May peace be upon him) and do according to his doing. We set out with him till we reached Dhu'l-Hulaifa. Asma' daughter of Umais gave birth to Muhammad b. Abu Bakr.

She sent a message to the Messenger of Allah (May peace be upon him) asking him: What should 1 do? He (the Holy Prophet) said: Take a bath, bandage your private parts and put on Ihram. The Messenger of Allah (May peace be upon him) then prayed in the mosque and then mounted al-Qaswa (his she-camel) and it stood erect with him on its back at al-Baida'. And I saw as far as I could see in front of me but riders and pedestrians, and also on my right and on my left and behind me like this. And the Messenger of Allah (may peace be upon him) was prominent among us and the (revelation) of the Holy Qur'an was descending upon him. And it is he who knows (its true) significance. And whatever he did, we also did that. He pronounced the Oneness of Allah (saying):" Labbaik,0 Allah, Labbaik, Labbaik. Thou hast no partner, praise and grace is Thine and the Sovereignty too; Thou hast no partner."

And the people also pronounced this Talbiya which they pronounce (today). The Messenger of Allah (May peace be upon him) did not reject anything out of it. But the Messenger of Allah (May peace. be upon him) adhered to his own Talbiya. Jabir (Allah be pleased with him) said: We did not have any other intention but that of Hajj only, being unaware of the Umra (at that season), but when we came with him to the House, he touched the pillar and (made seven circuits) running three of them and walking four. And then going to the Station of Ibrahim, he recited:" And adopt the Station of Ibrahim as a place of prayer." And this Station was between him and the House. My father said (and I do not know whether he had made a mention of it but that was from Allah's Apostle [May peace be upon him] that he recited in two rak'ahs:" say: He is Allah One," and say:" Say: 0 unbelievers." He then returned to the pillar (Hajar Aswad) and kissed it. He then went out of the gate to al-Safa' and as he reached near it he recited:" Al-Safa' and al-Marwa are among the signs appointed by Allah," (adding:) I begin with what Allah (has commanded me) to begin. He first mounted al-Safa' till he saw the House, and facing Qibla he declared the Oneness of Allah and glorified Him, and said:" There is no god but Allah, One, there is no partner with Him. His is the Sovereignty. to Him praise is due. and He is Powerful over everything. There is no god but Allah alone, Who fulfilled His promise, helped His servant and routed the confederates alone." He then made supplications in the course of saying such words three times. He then descended and walked towards al- Marwa, and when his feet came down in the bottom of the valley, he ran, and when he began to ascend he walked till he reached al-Marwa. There he did as he had done at al-Safa'. And when it was his last running at al-Marwa he said: If I had known beforehand what I have come to know afterwards, I would not have brought sacrificial animals and would have performed an 'Umra. So, he who among you has not the sacrificial animals with him should put off Ihram and treat it as an Umra. Suraqa b. Malik b. Ju'sham got up and said: Messenger of Allah, does it apply to the present year, or does it apply forever? Thereupon the Messenger of Allah (May peace be upon him) intertwined the fingers (of one hand) into another and said twice: The 'Umra has become incorporated in the Hajj (adding):" No, but for ever and ever." 'Ali (RA) came from Yemen with the sacrificial animals for the Prophet (May peace be upon him) and found Fatimah (Allah be pleased with her) to be one among those who had put off Ihram and had put on dyed clothes and had applied antimony. He (Hazrat Ali) showed disapproval to it, whereupon she said: My father has commanded me to do this. He (the narrator) said that 'Ali used to say in Iraq: I went to the Messenger of Allah (may peace be upon him) showing annoyance at Fatimah for what she had done, and asked the (verdict) of Allah's Messenger (may peace be upon him) regarding what she had narrated from him, and told him that I was angry with her, whereupon he said: She has told the truth, she has told the truth. (The Holy Prophet then asked 'Ali): What did you say when you undertook to go for Hajj? I ('Ali) said: 0 Allah, I am putting on Ihram for the same purpose as Thy Messenger has put it on.

He said: I have with me sacrificial animals, so do not put off the Ihram. He (Jabir) said: The total number of those sacrificial animals brought by 'Ali from Yemen and of those brought by the Apostle (may peace be upon him) was one hundred. Then all the people except the Apostle (may peace be upon him) and those who had with them sacrificial animals, put off Ihram, and got their hair clipped; when it was the day of Tarwiya (8th of Dhul-Hijjah) they went to Mina and put on the Ihram for Hajj and the Messenger of Ailah (may peace be upon him) rode and led the noon, afternoon, sunset 'Isha' and dawn prayers. He then waited a little till the sun rose, and commanded that a tent of hair should be pitched at Namira. The Messenger of Allah (may peace be upon him) then set out and the Quraish did not doubt that he would halt at al-Mash'ar al-Haram (the sacred site) as the Quraish used to do in the pre-Islamic period. The Messenger of Allah (may peace be upon him), however, passed on till he came to 'Arafa and he found that the tent had been pitched for him at Namira. There he got down till the sun had passed the meridian; he commanded that al-Qaswa should be brought and saddled for him. Then he came to the bottom of the valley, and addressed the people saying: Verily your blood, your property are as sacred and inviolable as the sacredness of this day of yours, in this month of yours, in this town of yours. Behold! Everything pertaining to the Days of Ignorance is under my feet completely abolished. Abolished are also the blood-revenges of the Days of Ignorance.

The first claim of ours on blood-revenge which I abolish is that of the son of Rabi'a b. al-Harith, who was nursed among the tribe of Sa'd and killed by Hudhail. And the usury of her pre-Islamic period is abolished, and the first of our usury I abolish is that of 'Abbas b. 'Abd al-Muttalib, for it is all abolished. Fear Allah concerning women! Verily you have taken them on the security of Allah, and intercourse with them has been made lawful unto you by words of Allah. You too have right over them, and that they should not allow anyone to sit on your bed whom you do not like. But if they do that, you can chastise them but not severely. Their rights upon you are that you should provide them with food and clothing in a fitting manner. I have left among you the Book of Allah, and if you hold fast to it, you would never go astray. And you would be asked about me (on the Day of Resurrection), (now tell me) what would you say? They (the audience) said: We will bear witness that you have conveyed (the message), discharged (the ministry of Prophethood) and given wise (sincere) counsel. He (the narrator) said: He (the Holy Prophet) then raised his forefinger towards the sky and pointed it at the people (said):" O Allah, be witness. 0 Allah, be witness," saying it thrice. (Bilal then) pronounced Adhan and later on Iqama and he (the Holy Prophet) led the noon prayer. He (Bilal) then uttered Iqama and he (the Holy Prophet) led the afternoon prayer and he observed no other prayer in between the two.

The Messenger of Allah (may peace be upon him) then mounted his camel and came to the place of stay, making his she-camel al-Qaswa, turn towards the side where there we are rocks, having the path taken by those who went on foot in front of him, and faced the Qibla. He kept standing there till the sun set, and the yellow light had somewhat gone, and the disc of the sun had disappeared. He made Usama sit behind him, and he pulled the nosestring of Qaswa so forcefully that its head touched the saddle (in order to keep her under perfect control), and he pointed out to the people with his right hand to be moderate (in speed), and whenever he happened to pass over an elevated tract of sand, he slightly loosened it (the nose-string of his camel) till she climbed up and this is how he reached al-Muzdalifa. There he led the evening and 'Isha prayers with one Adhan and two Iqamas and did not glorify (Allah) in between them (i. e. he did not observe supererogatory rak'ahs between Maghrib and 'Isha' prayers). The Messenger of Allah (may peace be upon him) then lay down till dawn and offered the dawn prayer with an Adhan and Iqama when the morning light was clear. He again mounted al-Qaswa, and when he came to al-Mash'ar al-Haram, he faced towards Qibla, supplicated Him, Glorified Him, and pronounced His Uniqueness (La ilaha illa Allah) and Oneness, and kept standing till the daylight was very clear.

He then went quickly before the sun rose, and seated behind him was al- Fadl b. 'Abbas and he was a man having beautiful hair and fair complexion and a handsome face. As the Messenger of Allah (May peace be upon him) was moving on, there was also a group of women (side by side with them). Al-Fadl began to look at them. The Messenger of Allah (may peace be upon him) placed his hand on the face of Fadl who then turned his face to the other side, and began to see, and the Messenger of Allah (may peace be upon him) turned his hand to the other side and placed it on the face of al-Fadl. He again turned his face to the other side till he came to the bottom of Muhassir. 1680 He urged her (al-Qaswa) a little, and, following the middle road, which comes out at the greatest jamra, he came to the jamra which is near the tree. At this be threw seven small pebbles, saying Allah-o- Akbar while throwing every one of them in a manner in which the small pebbles are thrown (with the help of fingers) and this he did in the bottom of the valley. He then went to the place of sacrifice, and sacrificed sixty-three (camels) with his own hand. Then he gave the remaining number to 'Ali who sacrificed them, and he shared him in his sacrifice. He then commanded that a piece of flesh from each animal sacrificed should be put in a pot, and when it was cooked, both of them (the Holy Prophet and Hadrat 'Ali) took some meat out of it and drank its soup. The Messenger of Allah (May peace be upon him) again rode and came to the House, and offered the Zuhr prayer at Mecca. He came to the tribe of Abd al- Muttalib, who was supplying water at Zamzam, and said: Draw water. O Bani 'Abd al-Muttalib; were it not that people would usurp this right of supplying water from you, I would have drawn it along with you. So they handed him a basket and he drank from it.

Sahih Muslim

Book 2, p. 253 #1218

While practice of deen in America has been fairly common for longer than generally recognized by most; the final pillar had not been experienced by Americans until the mid to late twentieth century. Malcolm x was among the few who traveled from America to perform Hajj during the early period in the mid-20th century (1964) but it was, not until the 1980s when immigration of people from Muslim countries became a reality that hajj from America became a common event... first among the immigrant communities, followed by the indigenous Americans populations.

Attending hajj in 1983 with brothers from the DAR movement and other New York residents, this writer's experience was phenomenal in that the "Muslim World" was so different from anything previously touched and interaction with people from a vast cultural landscape, left an indelible portrait on my psyche. Similar to the Hajj experiences that were portrayed for Malcolm X, in his Autobiography; my Hajj experience was a major eye opener, wake up call, historic event. Seeing people looking like many of those we would encounter in our own neighborhoods and realizing that they were from somewhere else once they spoke, it began to become clear that we are really all the same, just separated by space and language

We were housed in a facility where we spread out our rug In an area where each culture, nationality, language were together.

Americans were still fairly rare visitors. and special. I recall after briefly speaking asking directions etc. with a person who lived in the area of the kabba, being spotlighted to others nearby by him as "Amreek" as if the presence of an Amreek/American was a major event. to others there. At the time Americans were a fairly new commodity valued and respected and especially those of us that resembled the people who lived there in the region. Also, like Malcolm x, my performance of the prescribed rituals and touching the black stone and drinking from the well of Zam-zam which was discovered by Hagar as she ran between the mountains searching for water to nourish her son, Ishmael, transported my spirit and mind to more than a thousand years into places described in scriptures.

Upon return to home my efforts to describe the Hajj experience were not easy. It took a while to download all of the mental and spiritual messages received to a point where I could practice and share them.

Evolution of world Religion

Shahadatain

Islam is based on Tauhid -worship of God alone without partnership and total submission. Allah spoke to Moses in the Old Testament calling to the oneness of Allah.

Numbers 15:37-41 King James Version (KJV)

37 And the Lord spake unto Moses, saying,38 Speak unto the children of Israel, and bid them that they make them fringes in the borders of their garments throughout their generations, and that they put upon the fringe of the borders a ribband of blue: 39 And it shall be unto you for a fringe, that ye may look upon it, and remember all the commandments of the Lord, and do them; and that ye seek not after your own heart and your own eyes, after which ye use to go a whoring: 40 That ye may remember, and do all my commandments, and be holy unto your God. 41 I am the Lord your God, which brought you out of the land of Egypt, to be your God: I am the Lord your God.

Deuteronomy 6:4-9 New King James Version (NKJV)

4 "Hear, O Israel: The Lord our God, the Lord *is* one! 5 You shall love the Lord your God with all your heart, with all your soul, and with

all your strength. 6 "And these words which I command you today shall be in your heart. 7 You shall teach them diligently to your children, and shall talk of them when you sit in your house, when you walk by the way, when you lie down, and when you rise up. 8 You shall bind them as a sign on your hand, and they shall be as frontlets between your eyes. 9 You shall write them on the doorposts of your house and on your gates.

Jesus (AS) told us in the New Testament about Tauhid

Matthew 22:34-40 King James Version (KJV)

34 But when the Pharisees had heard that he had put the Sadducees to silence, they were gathered together. 35 Then one of them, which was a lawyer, asked him a question, tempting him, and saying,36 Master, which is the great commandment in the law? 37 Jesus said unto him, Thou shalt love the Lord thy God with all thy heart, and with all thy soul, and with all thy mind. 38 This is the first and great commandment. 39 And the second is like unto it, Thou shalt love thy neighbour as thyself. 40 On these two commandments hang all the law and the prophets.

Mark 12:28-34 King James Version (KJV)

28 And one of the scribes came, and having heard them reasoning together, and perceiving that he had answered them well, asked him, Which is the first commandment of all? 29 And Jesus answered him, The first of all the commandments is, Hear, O Israel; The Lord our God is one Lord: 30 And thou shalt love the Lord thy God with all thy heart, and with all thy soul, and with all thy mind, and with all thy strength: this is the first commandment. 31 And the second is like, namely this, Thou shalt love thy neighbour as thyself. There is none other commandment greater than these. 32 And the scribe said unto him, Well, Master, thou

hast said the truth: for there is one God; and there is none other but he: 33 And to love him with all the heart, and with all the understanding, and with all the soul, and with all the strength, and to love his neighbour as himself, is more than all whole burnt offerings and sacrifices. 34 And when Jesus saw that he answered discreetly, he said unto him, Thou art not far from the kingdom of God. And no man after that durst asked him any question.

Matthew 4:1-11 NIV

1. Then Jesus was led by the Spirit into the wilderness to be tempted by the devil. 2 After fasting forty days and forty nights, he was hungry.3 The tempter came to him and said, "If you are the Son of God, tell these stones to become bread." 4 Jesus answered, "It is written: 'Man shall not live on bread alone, but on every word that comes from the mouth of God.'" 5 Then the devil took him to the holy city and had him stand on the highest point of the temple. 6 "If you are the Son of God," he said, "throw yourself down. For it is written:

"'He will command his angels concerning you,

and they will lift you up in their hands,

so that you will not strike your foot against a stone.'"

7 Jesus answered him, "It is also written: 'Do not put the Lord your God to the test.'"

8 Again, the devil took him to a very high mountain and showed him all the kingdoms of the world and their splendor. 9 "All this I will give you," he said, "if you will bow down and worship me." 10 Jesus said to him, "Away from me, Satan! For it is written: 'Worship the Lord your God, and serve him only.'" 11 Then the devil left him, and angels came and attended him.

Matthew 23:8-12 King James Version (KJV)

8 But be not ye called Rabbi: for one is your Master, even Christ; and all ye are brethren.

9 And call no man your father upon the earth: for one is your Father, which is in heaven.

10 Neither be ye called masters: for one is your Master, even Christ. 11 But he that is greatest among you shall be your servant. 12 And whosoever shall exalt himself shall be abased; and he that shall humble himself shall be exalted.

Allah said in the Quran Surah 4 AnNisa **36. Worship Allah and associate nothing with Him, and to parents do good, and to relatives, orphans, the needy, the near neighbor, the neighbor farther away, the companion at your side, the traveler, and those whom your right hands possess. Indeed, Allah does not like those who are self-deluding and boastful.**

<u>*Prayer*</u>

Prayer (Salaat) in the Bible where David (AS) lead his community in prayer

1 Chronicles 29:10-20 King James Version (KJV)

10 Wherefore David blessed the Lord before all the congregation: and David said, Blessed be thou, Lord God of Israel our father, for ever and ever. 11 Thine, O Lord is the greatness, and the power, and the glory, and the victory, and the majesty: for all that is in heaven and in the earth is thine; thine is the kingdom, O Lord, and thou art exalted as head above

all. 12 Both riches and honour come of thee, and thou reignest over all; and in thine hand is power and might; and in thine hand it is to make great, and to give strength unto all. 13 Now therefore, our God, we thank thee, and praise thy glorious name. 14 But who am I, and what are my people, that we should be able to offer so willingly after this sort? for all things come of thee, and of thine own have we given thee. 15 For we are strangers before thee, and sojourners, as were all our fathers: our days on the earth are as a shadow, and there is none abiding. 16 O Lord our God, all this store that we have prepared to build thee an house for thine holy name cometh of thine hand, and is all thine own. 17 I know also, my God, that thou triest the heart, and hast pleasure in uprightness. As for me, in the uprightness of mine heart I have willingly offered all these things: and now have I seen with joy thy people, which are present here, to offer willingly unto thee. 18 O Lord God of Abraham, Isaac, and of Israel, our fathers, keep this for ever in the imagination of the thoughts of the heart of thy people, and prepare their heart unto thee: 19 And give unto Solomon my son a perfect heart, to keep thy commandments, thy testimonies, and thy statutes, and to do all these things, and to build the palace, for the which I have made provision. 20 And David said to all the congregation, Now bless the Lord your God. And all the congregation blessed the Lord God of their fathers, and bowed down their heads, and worshipped the Lord, and the king.

Moses and Aaron prayed (offered Salat) asking for water

Numbers 20:4-8 King James Version (KJV)

4 And why have ye brought up the congregation of the Lord into this wilderness, that we and our cattle should die there? 5 And wherefore have ye made us to come up out of Egypt, to bring us in unto this evil place? it is no place of seed, or of figs, or of vines, or of

pomegranates; neither is there any water to drink. 6 And Moses and Aaron went from the presence of the assembly unto the door of the tabernacle of the congregation, and they fell upon their faces: and the glory of the Lord appeared unto them. 7 And the Lord spake unto Moses, saying,8 Take the rod, and gather thou the assembly together, thou, and Aaron thy brother, and speak ye unto the rock before their eyes; and it shall give forth his water, and thou shalt bring forth to them water out of the rock: so thou shalt give the congregation and their beasts drink.

Jesus prayed (offered Salat) in his time of distress

Matthew 26:36-39 King James Version (KJV)

36 Then cometh Jesus with them unto a place called Gethsemane, and saith unto the disciples, Sit ye here, while I go and pray yonder. 37 And he took with him Peter and the two sons of Zebedee, and began to be sorrowful and very heavy. 38 Then saith he unto them, My soul is exceeding sorrowful, even unto death: tarry ye here, and watch with me. 39 And he went a little farther, and fell on his face, and prayed, saying, O my Father, if it be possible, let this cup pass from me: nevertheless not as I will, but as thou wilt.

Allah telling us that Prayer is a characteristic of the Believers

Allah said in Surah 23 Al Mu'mimneen 1-10 **Successful indeed are the believers (1) Who are humble in their prayers, (2) And who shun vain conversation, (3) And who are payers of the poor-due; (4) And who guard their modesty (5) Save from their wives or the (slaves) that their right hands possess, for then they are not blameworthy, (6) But whoso craveth beyond that, such are transgressors (7) And who are keepers of their pledge and their covenant, (8) And who pay heed to** their prayers. (9) These are the heirs (10) Who will inherit paradise. There they will abide.

Charity

God tells Moses to inform the Israelites to give Charity

Exodus 25:1-8 King James Version (KJV)

1 And the Lord spake unto Moses, saying, 2 Speak unto the children of Israel, that they bring me an offering: of every man that giveth it willingly with his heart ye shall take my offering. 3 And this is the offering which ye shall take of them; gold, and silver, and brass, 4 And blue, and purple, and scarlet, and fine linen, and goats' hair, 5 And rams' skins dyed red, and badgers' skins, and shittim wood, 6 Oil for the light, spices for anointing oil, and for sweet incense, 7 Onyx stones, and stones to be set in the ephod, and in the breastplate. 8 And let them make me a sanctuary; that I may dwell among them.

Jesus tells a man give Charity to obtain eternal Life

Matthew 19:16-22 King James Version (KJV)

16 And, behold, one came and said unto him, Good Master, what good thing shall I do, that I may have eternal life? 17 And he said unto him, Why callest thou me good? there is none good but one, that is, God: but if thou wilt enter into life, keep the commandments. 18 He saith unto him, Which? Jesus said, Thou shalt do no murder, Thou shalt not commit adultery, Thou shalt not steal, Thou shalt not bear false witness, 19 Honour thy father and thy mother: and, Thou shalt love thy neighbour as thyself. 20 The young man saith unto him, All these things have I kept from my youth up: what lack I yet? 21 Jesus said unto him,

If thou wilt be perfect, go and sell that thou hast, and give to the poor, and thou shalt have treasure in heaven: and come and follow me. 22 But when the young man heard that saying, he went away sorrowful: for he had great possessions.

Islam is the Natural Progression

Ibn Abbas reported: When the Messenger of Allah, peace and blessings be upon him, sent Mu'adh to Yemen, he said to him:

إِنَّكَ تَأْتِي قَوْمًا مِنْ أَهْلِ الْكِتَابِ فَادْعُهُمْ إِلَى شَهَادَةِ أَنْ لَا إِلَهَ إِلَّا اللَّهُ وَأَنِّي رَسُولُ اللَّهِ فَإِنْ هُمْ أَطَاعُوا لِذَلِكَ فَأَعْلِمْهُمْ أَنَّ اللَّهَ افْتَرَضَ عَلَيْهِمْ خَمْسَ صَلَوَاتٍ فِي كُلِّ يَوْمٍ وَلَيْلَةٍ فَإِنْ هُمْ أَطَاعُوا لِذَلِكَ فَأَعْلِمْهُمْ أَنَّ اللَّهَ افْتَرَضَ عَلَيْهِمْ صَدَقَةً تُؤْخَذُ مِنْ أَغْنِيَائِهِمْ فَتُرَدُّ فِي فُقَرَائِهِمْ فَإِنْ هُمْ أَطَاعُوا لِذَلِكَ فَإِيَّاكَ وَكَرَائِمَ أَمْوَالِهِمْ وَاتَّقِ دَعْوَةَ الْمَظْلُومِ فَإِنَّهُ لَيْسَ بَيْنَهَا وَبَيْنَ اللَّهِ حِجَابٌ

Verily, you are coming to a people among the people of the Book (Jews and Christians), so call them to testify there is no God but Allah and I am the Messenger of Allah. If they accept that, then teach them that Allah has obligated five prayers in each day and night. If they accept that, then teach them that Allah has obligated charity to be taken from the rich and given to the poor. If they accept that, beware not to take from the best of their wealth. Be on guard from the supplication of the oppressed, for there is no barrier between it and Allah.

Source: Sahih Muslim 19, Grade: Muttafaqun Alayhi

Mentions of the coming of Prophet Muhammad

Moses tells his community to follow Muhammad

Deuteronomy 18:14-22 King James Version (KJV)

14 For these nations, which thou shalt possess, hearkened unto observers of times, and unto diviners: but as for thee, the Lord thy God hath not suffered thee so to do. 15 The Lord thy God will raise up unto thee a Prophet from the midst of thee, of thy brethren, like unto me; unto him ye shall hearken; 16 According to all that thou desirest of the Lord thy God in Horeb in the day of the assembly, saying, Let me not hear again the voice of the Lord My God, neither let me see this great fire any more, that I die not. 17 And the Lord said unto me, They have well spoken that which they have spoken. 18 I will raise them up a Prophet from among their brethren, like unto thee, and will put my words in his mouth; and he shall speak unto them all that I shall command him. 19 And it shall come to pass, that whosoever will not hearken unto my words which he shall speak in my name, I will require it of him. 20 But the prophet, which shall presume to speak a word in my name, which I have not commanded him to speak, or that shall speak in the name of other gods, even that prophet shall die. 21 And if thou say in thine heart, How shall we know the word which the Lord hath not spoken? 22 When

a prophet speaketh in the name of the Lord, if the thing follows not, nor come to pass, that is the thing which the Lord hath not spoken, but the prophet hath spoken it presumptuously: thou shalt not be afraid of him.

And

Acts 3:22-26 King James Version (KJV)

22 For Moses truly said unto the fathers, A prophet shall the Lord your God raise up unto you of your brethren, like unto me; him shall ye hear in all things whatsoever he shall say unto you. 23 And it shall come to pass, that every soul, which will not hear that prophet, shall be destroyed from among the people. 24 Yea, and all the prophets from Samuel and those that follow after, as many as have spoken, have likewise foretold of these days. 25 Ye are the children of the prophets, and of the covenant which God made with our fathers, saying unto Abraham, And in thy seed shall all the kindreds of the earth be blessed.

John is not the Christ, the Prophet, or Elijah but who is that Prophet who obviously came after Jesus? _____

John 1:19-28 King James Version (KJV)

19 And this is the record of John, when the Jews sent priests and Levites from Jerusalem to ask him, Who art thou? 20 And he confessed, and denied not; but confessed, I am not the Christ. 21 And they asked him, What then? Art thou Elias? And he saith, I am not. Art thou that prophet? And he answered, No. 22 Then said they unto him, Who art thou? that we may give an answer to them that sent us. What sayest thou of thyself? 23 He said, I am the voice of one crying in the wilderness, Make straight the way of the Lord, as said the prophet Esaias. 24 And they which were sent were of the Pharisees. 25 And they asked him, and

said unto him, Why baptizest thou then, if thou be not that Christ, nor Elias, neither that prophet? 26 John answered them, saying, I baptize with water: but there standeth one among you, whom ye know not; 27 He it is, who coming after me is preferred before me, whose shoe's latchet I am not worthy to unloose. 28 These things were done in Bethabara beyond Jordan, where John was baptizing.

Jesus tell his community to follow Muhammad

John 14:15-16 King James Version (KJV)

15 If ye love me, keep my commandments. 16 And I will pray the Father, and he shall give you another Comforter, that he may abide with you forever;

Muslim theologians have said that "another Comforter" is Muhammad, the Messenger of Allah; and him to "abide forever" means the perpetuity of his laws and way of life (Shari'ah) and the Book (Qur'an) which was revealed to him.

John 15:26-27 King James Version (KJV)

26 But when the Comforter is come, whom I will send unto you from the Father, even the Spirit of truth, which proceedeth from the Father, he shall testify of me: 27 And ye also shall bear witness, because ye have been with me from the beginning.

John 16:5-8 King James Version (KJV)

5 But now I go my way to him that sent me; and none of you asketh me, Whither goest thou? 6 But because I have said these things unto you, sorrow hath filled your heart. 7 Nevertheless I tell you the truth; It is expedient for

you that I go away: for if I go not away, the Comforter will not come unto you; but if I depart, I will send him unto you. 8 And when he is come, he will reprove the world of sin, and of righteousness, and of judgment:

John 16:12-14 King James Version (KJV)

12. I have yet many things to say unto you, but ye cannot bear them now. 13. Howbeit when he, the Spirit of truth, is come, he will guide you into all truth: for he shall not speak of himself; but whatsoever he shall hear, that shall he speak: and he will shew you things to come. 14. He shall glorify me: for he shall receive of mine, and shall shew it unto you.

This person whom Jesus prophesied will come after him is called in the Bible 'Parqaleeta' This word was deleted by later interpreters and translators and changed at times to 'Spirit of Truth' and at other times, to 'Comforter' and sometimes to 'Holy Spirit'. The original word is Greek and its meaning is 'one whom people praise exceedingly'.

Many Muslim writers have argued that "another Paraclete" (John 14:16)—the first being Jesus—refers to Muhammad. This claim is based on the Quran verse from Surah 61 verse 6. The earliest scholar to argue this case is probably Ibn Ishaq (died 767), who Islamic tradition states was the grandson of a Christian. Others who interpreted the paraclete as a reference to Muhammad include Ibn Taymiyyah, Ibn Kathir, Al-Qurtubi, and Rahmatullah Kairanawi (1818–1891).

Allah said

Surat 61 As-Saff 6: **"And [mention] when Jesus, the son of Mary, said, "O children of Israel, indeed I am the messenger of Allah to you confirming what came before me of the Torah and bringing good tidings of a messenger to come after me, whose name is Ahmad." But when he came to them with clear evidences, they said, "This is obvious magic."**

Allah said

Surah 7 Al-A'raf 157. **Those who follow the Messenger, the unlettered prophet, whom they find written in what they have of the Torah (Deut, xviii,15) and the Gospel (John xiv, 16), who enjoins upon them what is right and forbids them what is wrong and makes lawful for them the good things and prohibits for them the evil and relieves them of their burden and the shackles which were upon them. So they who have believed in him, honored him, supported him and followed the light which was sent down with him - it is those who will be the successful.**

Deuteronomy 18:15 King James Version (KJV)

15 The Lord thy God will raise up unto thee a Prophet from the midst of thee, of thy brethren, like unto me; unto him ye shall hearken;

Allah said

Surah 4 AnNisa 47. **O you who were given the Scripture, believe in what We have sent down [to Muhammad], confirming that which is with you, before We obliterate faces and turn them toward their backs or curse them as We cursed the sabbath-breakers. And ever is the decree of Allah accomplished.**

The islamic Dress code

1 Corinthians 11:4-7 King James Version (KJV)

4 Every man praying or prophesying, having his head covered, dishonoureth his head. 5 But every woman that prayeth or prophesieth with her head uncovered dishonoureth her head: for that is even all one

99

as if she were shaven. 6 For if the woman be not covered, let her also be shorn: but if it be a shame for a woman to be shorn or shaven, let her be covered. 7 For a man indeed ought not to cover his head, forasmuch as he is the image and glory of God: but the woman is the glory of the man.

Allah Said

Surah 33 Al Ahzab 59. **O Prophet, enjoin your wives and your daughters and the believing women, to draw a part of their outer coverings around them. It is likelier that they will be recognised and not molested. Allah is Most Forgiving, Most Merciful.**

Faith Without Works Is Dead

James 2:14-26 New King James Version (NKJV)

14 What does it profit, my brethren, if someone says he has faith but does not have works? Can faith save him? 15 If a brother or sister is naked and destitute of daily food, 16 and one of you says to them, "Depart in peace, be warmed and filled," but you do not give them the things which are needed for the body, what does it profit? 17 Thus also faith by itself, if it does not have works, is dead. 18 But someone will say, "You have faith, and I have work." Show me your faith without your works, and I will show you my faith by my works. 19 You believe that there is one God. You do well. Even the demons believe and tremble! 20 But do you want to know, O foolish man, that faith without works is dead? 21 Was not Abraham our father justified by works when he offered Isaac his son on the altar? 22 Do you see that faith was working together with his works, and by works faith was made perfect? 23 And the Scripture was fulfilled which says, "Abraham believed God, and it was accounted to him for righteousness." And he was called the friend of God. 24 You see

then that a man is justified by works, and not by faith only. 25 Likewise, was not Rahab the harlot also justified by works when she received the messengers and sent them out another way? 26 For as the body without the spirit is dead, so faith without works is dead also.

Have Faith and Do righteous good deeds

Surah An-Nisa' 4: Ayah 124

And whoever does righteous good deeds, male or female, and is a (true) believer, such will enter Paradise and not the least injustice, even to the size of a speck on the back of a date-stone, will be done to them.

Surah Al-Maidah 5: Ayah 9

Allah has promised those who believe and do deeds of righteousness that for them there is forgiveness and a great reward (i.e. Paradise).

Surah Yunus 10: Ayah 9

Verily, those who believe, and do deeds of righteousness, their Lord will guide them through their faith; under them will flow rivers in the Gardens of Delight (Paradise).

Surah Hud 11: Ayah 11

Except those who show patience and do righteous good deeds: those, there will be forgiveness and a great reward (Paradise).

Surah Hud 11: Ayah 23

Verily, those who believe and do righteous good deeds, and humble themselves before their Lord, they will be dwellers of Paradise To dwell therein forever.

Surah Al-Kahf 18: Ayat 30 – 31

Verily as for those who believed and did righteous deeds, certainly We shall not make the reward of anyone who does his (righteous deeds in the most perfect manner to be lost. These! For them will be Adn (Eden) Paradise (everlasting Gardens); wherein rivers flow underneath them; therein they will be adorned with bracelets of gold, and they will wear green garments of fine and thick silk. They will reclinetherein on raised thrones. How good is the reward, and what an excellent Muttafaq (dwelling, resting place.)!

Surah Al-Kahf 18: Ayah 107

Verily those who believe and do righteous deeds shall have the Gardens of Al-Firdaus (Paradise) for their entertainment.

Surah Al-Hajj 22: Ayah 14

Truly, Allah will admit those who believe and do righteous good deeds to Gardens Underneath which rivers flow (in Paradise). Verily, Allah does what He wills.

Surah Al-Hajj 22: Ayah 23.

Truly, Allah will admit those who believe and do righteous good deeds, to Gardens Underneath which rivers flow (in Paradise), wherein they will be adorned with bracelets of gold and pearls and their garments there will be of silk.

Surah Al-Hajj 22: Ayah 50

So those who believe and do righteous good deeds, for them is forgiveness and Rizqun Karim (generous provision, i.e. Paradise).

Surah Luqman 31: Ayah 8

Verily, those who believe and do righteous good deeds, for them are Gardens of Delight(paradise).

Surah Saba 34: Ayah 4

That He may recompense those who believe and do righteous good deeds. Those, theirs is forgiveness and Rizq karim (generous provision, i.e. Paradise).

Surah Fatir 35: Ayah 7

… and those who believe and do righteous good deeds, theirs will be forgiveness and agreat reward (i.e. Paradise).

Surah Fussilat 41: Ayah 8

Truly, those who believe and do righteous good deeds, for them will be an endless reward that will never stop (i.e. Paradise).

Surah Ash-Shura 42: Ayah 22

… But those who believe and do righteous deeds (will be) in the flowering meadows of the Gardens (Paradise). They shall have whatsoever they desire with their Lord. That Is the supreme grace, (Paradise).

Surah Al-Jathiya 45: Ayah 30

Then, as for those who believed and did righteous good deeds, their Lord will admit them to His Mercy. That will be the evident success.

Surah Muhammad 47: Ayah 2

But those who believe and do righteous good deeds, and believe in that which is sent down to Muhammad (salla allahu alayhi wa salaam) for it is the truth from their Lord– He will expiate from them their sins, andwill make good their state.

Surah At-Taghabun 64: Ayah 9

... And whosoever believes in Allah and performs righteous good deeds, He will expiate from him his sins, and will admit him to Gardens under which rivers flow(Paradise) to dwell therein forever; that will be the great success.

Surah At-Tin 95: Ayah 6

Save those who believe and do righteous deeds. Then they shall have a reward without end(Paradise).

Surah Al-Bayyinah 98: Ayah 7-8

Verily, those who believe and do righteous good deeds, they are the best of creatures. Their reward with their Lord is 'Adn (Eden) Paradise (Gardens of eternity), underneath which rivers flow. They will abide therein forever, Allah will be pleased with them, and they with Him. That is for him who fears his Lord.

Once one can agree that the 5 pillars or principle of Islam are not new concepts but they originate from Abraham and can be found all throught the Torah and Bible, You may know that Islam is Right for you. I dont want to give the indication that by just becoming a Muslim that all your problems will go away and all your dreams will come truebut I will say your reaction to lifes changes will be understandable. When things become too much to bear we simply beg God for his help and follow the practices of the Prophet out of our complications.

One of the best ways to worship Allah in the correct way is to get Married and have children. Family is the most important thing in Islam and distroying the family is directly related to the devil. So we are encouraged to marry the loving and prolific woman and be good to our Family.

Nikah (Marriage)

The sunnah of Nikah (Marriage) is of the utmost importance in Islam as it is ibadah (an act of worship). Marriage is so important that we can marry muslims or the men can marry muslims or the chaste women of the book (Jews and Christians). Many understand Marriage as wajib (an Obligatory act) because of the way Allah refers to it in the Quran and because of the emphasis placed on Marriage by the Prophet(ﷺ).

Allah said in Surah 24 ayat 32. **And marry the unmarried among you and the righteous among your male slaves and female slaves. If they should be poor, Allah will enrich them from His bounty, and Allah is all-Encompassing and Knowing.**

And as for the Sunnah

Narrated Anas bin Malik: A group of three men came to the houses of the wives of the Prophet asking how the Prophet worshipped (Allah), and when they were informed about that, they considered their worship insufficient and said, Where are we from the Prophet as his past and future sins have been forgiven. Then one of them said, I will offer prayer throughout the night forever. The other said, I will fast throughout the year and will not break my fast. The third said, I will keep away from the women and will not marry forever. Allah's Apostle came to them and said, Are you the same people who said so-and-so? By Allah, I am more submissive to Allah and more afraid of Him than you; yet I fast and break my fast, I do sleep and I also marry women. So he who does not follow my tradition in religion, is not from me (not one of my followers).

Sahih Al Bukhari 1: Chapter 68, Hadith 5063

So a clear instruction was giving to those Walli's (Guardians who are charged over the protection of the women{Fathers, Brothers, Imaam[religious leaders]}) by Allah, who is All-Encompassing All-Knowing, to marry the men and women under his care whether they be free believers or slaves and Allah will provide for them. In addition, The prophet tells us that if we become an extremist in worship by praying all night every night without giving your body its rights, giving your wife her rights, and then giving your lord his rights your not muslim. Being extreme in fasting everyday is also not allowed in islam, as the most a person can fast is the fast of Dawad (every other day) but we are suggested to fast the 14th, 15, and 16th (the 3 white nights), and mondays and thursdays, and of course the fast of the Month of Ramadan is obligatory. Anyone who exceeds the limits of fasting (Like the fast of the followers of Gandi) is not a muslim. Those who become extreme in worship by not marrying Women or women not marrying men (like the priest and nuns) are not Muslims. Allah's Messenger (ﷺ) also instructions our youth to Marry as,

Narrated `Abdullah: We were with the Prophet while we were young and had no wealth whatever. So Allah's Apostle said, O young people! Whoever among you can marry, should marry, because it helps him lower his gaze and guard his modesty (i.e. his private parts from committing illegal sexual intercourse etc.), and whoever is not able to marry, should fast, as fasting diminishes his sexual power.

Sahih Al Bukhari #5066

And as we go on the journey to increasing our levels from Islam(Total Submissionto Allah) to Iman (Faith) to Is'han (Perfection) without getting Married we only can complete half of our deen as,

Al-Bayhaqi narrated in Shu'ab al-Eemaan from al-Raqaashi: "When a person gets married he has completed half of his religion, so let him fear Allaah with regard to the other half.

"Al-Albaani said of this hadith in Saheeh al-Targheeb wa'l-Tarheeb (1916):

"(They are) hasan li ghayrihi." And if that is not enough of a proof and evidence for us to Get Married then let us look at all of the Prophets from Adam (AS) all the way to Muhammad (ﷺ), practically all of them were married. Allah only tells us specifics about 25 or 26 Prophets in the Quran:Adam, Idris (Enoch), Nuh (Noah), Hud (Heber), Saleh (Methusaleh), Lut (Lot), Ibrahim (Abraham), Ismail (Ishmael), Ishaq (Isaac), Yaqub (Jacob), Yusuf (Joseph), Shu'aib (Jethro), Ayyub (Job), Dhulkifl (Ezekiel), Musa (Moses), Harun (Aaron), Dawud, and possibly Khidr, (David), Sulayman (Solomon), Ilyas (Elias), Alyasa (Elisha), Yunus (Jonah), Zakariya (Zachariah), Yahya (John the Baptist), Isa (Jesus) and Muhammad. Peace be upon them all.

Allah said about Adam (AS) in Surah AnNisa Ayat 1. **O mankind! reverence your Guardian-Lord, who created you from a single person, created, of like nature, His mate, and from them twain scattered (like seeds) countless men and women;- reverence Allah, through whom ye demand your mutual (rights), and (reverence) the wombs (That bore you): for Allah ever watches over you.**

Allah tells us about Noah (AS) and Lut (AS) in Surah At-Tahrim 66:10: **"Allah has given examples of disbelievers: the wives of Nuh [Noah] and Lut [Lot] who married two of Our righteous servants, but** betrayed them. Their husbands could not help them against God: it was said,'Both of you enter the Fire with the others."

As for solomon, Abu Hurayrah who said: "Sulaymaan ibn Dawood (peace be upon them both) said: 'Tonight I will go around to one hundred wives, each of whom will give birth to a boy who will fight for the sake of Allah.' The angel said to him, 'Say in sha Allah (if Allaah wills).' But he did not say it, as he forgot. He went around to them but none of them gave birth, apart from one wife who gave birth to half a child. The Prophet (peace and blessings of Allaah be upon him) said: 'If he had said in sha Allah, he would not have broken his oath and he would have had more hope of fulfilling his wish.'"

Narrated by Muslim, 1654) Narrated by al-Bukhaari in his Saheeh (5242)

Allah tells us about Moses in Surah 28 Al Qasas ayat 26 **Then one of the two women came to him walking with shyness. She said, "Indeed, my father invites you that he may reward you for having watered for us." So when he came to him and related to him the story, he said, "Fear not. You have escaped from the wrongdoing people."27. One of the women said, "O my father, hire him. Indeed, the best one you can hire is the strong and the trustworthy."28. He said, "Indeed, I wish to wed you one of these, my two daughters, on [the condition] that you serve me for eight years; but if you complete ten, it will be [as a favor] from you. And I do not wish to put you in difficulty. You will find me, if Allah wills, from among the righteous."**

As for Rusullullah (ﷺ) he had several wives from a variety of types of women being as though he is the last and final prophet. His (ﷺ) duty was more severe to ensure humanity received the message Allah was sending through all of the prophets. So we learn how to deal with our wifes who are older than us. We learn how to deal with wifes who have more wealth than us. We learn how to deal with our women when they become jealous. We also learn how to teach our wives and also take advice from them, and much more.

Anas (may Allah be pleased with him), who said: The Prophet (blessings and peace of Allah be upon him) had nine wives, and when he divided his time among them, he did not come back to the first one until the ninth day. Every night they used to gather in the house of the one whose night it was. He was in 'Aa'ishah's house, and Zaynab came and he reached out his hand towards her. 'Aa'ishah said: This is Zaynab, and the Prophet (blessings and peace of Allah be upon him) withdrew his hand. They argued and raised their voices, and the iqaamah for prayer was given. Abu Bakr came past at that point and heard their voices, so he said: Come out for the prayer, O Messenger of Allah, and throw dust in their mouths. The Prophet (blessings and peace of Allah be upon him) came out, and 'Aa'ishah said: Now the Prophet (blessings and peace of Allah be upon him) will finish his prayer and come, and Abu Bakr will come and do such and such to me. When the Prophet (blessings and peace of Allah be upon him) had finished his prayer, Abu Bakr came to her and spoke sternly to her, and said: Do you behave like this?

Narrated by Muslim (1462)

Many of the Prophets of the past practiced Polygynous Marriage as I already mentioned Rasullullah(ﷺ) and Sulaymaan ibn Dawood (AS), but also his Father Dawood (AS), Ibrahim (AS) and Jacob (AS) according to the isrealite sources. With the coming of the Messenger of Allah (ﷺ) and his sharii'ah Allah limited the number of wives to four

Allah said in Surah An Nisa 3. **And if you fear that you shall not be able to deal justly with the orphan-girls, then marry (other) women of your choice, two or three, or four but if you fear that you shall not** be able to deal justly (with them), then only one or (the captives and the slaves) that your right hands possess. That is nearer to preventing you from doing injustice.

Islam requires the man who has more than one wife to treat his wives equally and fairly. What is meant by that is fairness with regard to spending the night, accommodation, spending and clothing.

Al-Shaafa'i said:

The Sunnah of the Messenger of Allah (ﷺ) and the view of most of the Muslim scholars indicate that the man must divide his time, night and day, among his wives, and must divide it equally, and that he is not allowed to be unfair in that. However Love (feeling) is not something we have control over so

Allah said in Surah 4 An Nisa 129. **And you will never be able to be equal [in feeling] between wives, even if you should strive [to do so]. So do not incline completely [toward one] and leave another hanging. And if you amend [your affairs] and fear Allah - then indeed, Allah is ever Forgiving and Merciful.**

Narrated Aishah, Ummul Muminin: The Messenger of Allah صلى الله عليه وسلم used to divide his time equally and said: O Allah, this is my division concerning what I control, so do not blame me concerning what You control and I do not. Abu Dawud said: By it meant the heart.

Sunah Abu Dawood hadith no. 2134

Allah said in Surah 13 Ar Ra'd 38. **We did send messengers before thee, and appointed for them wives and children: and it was never**

the part of a messenger to bring a sign except as Allah permitted (or commanded). For each period is a Book (revealed).

Of course there were prophets no information about being married was found in the Qur'an or authentic Sunnah. For example Yahya (John the Baptist [AS]) and Isa Jesus (AS) where never married

Allah said in Surah 3 Ali Imran 39. **While he was standing in prayer in the chamber, the angels called unto him: "Allah doth give thee glad tidings of Yahya, witnessing the truth of a Word from Allah, and (be besides) noble, chaste, and a prophet,- of the (goodly) company of the righteous."**

As we are inheritors of the prophets we too should follow them in marriage as it is one of the greatest acts of worship. So much so that the scholars say when Isa Ibn Maryam descends he will get married, have children and eventually die as he has not been crucified. Many don't get married these days for a number of reasons and this clearly explains the condition we are in as a humanity. The Fitnah and Fasad (tribulation and corruptions) we endure in our society is directly related to marriage or the lack thereof. Zina (illegal sexual intercourse) is a common practice often resulting in children of the bed, And ask yourself what is the ratio of troubled youth without men in the home? How many of those children are causing this corruption that we see every day because they have no male role model? How many of them find their ways into jail. Some result in depression or even suicidal. Just look at the condition of our youth today. Our muslim women dating non Muslim Men, Homosexuality is at an all time high, intoxication of drugs and Alcohol is common in our communities, ignorance is prevalent as we see with the distruction of our neighborhood by the residence who live there. Everyone is giving their opinion on a topic where they have no knowledge and even worse they dont judge by the Quran. For example beneficial knowledge is not necessarily to indulge in everything people do in this Dunya. Beneficial knowledge is what Allah says and what the Prophet says, because these are the things that will benefit you in this life and the next. Beneficial knowledge to me is to know about the month of Shawwal and How did the prophet treat this month?

'Aa'ishah (may Allaah be pleased with her) said: "The Messenger of Allaah (peace and blessings of Allaah be upon him) married me in Shawwaal and consummated the marriage with me in Shawwaal, and which of his wives was more favoured by him than me?"

(Narrated by Ahmad in al-Musnad, 6/54; this version narrated by him. Also narrated by

Muslim in his Saheeh

So we as muslims should not wait for their pagan holidays of Love "Valentines Day" to make marriage important the prophet made marriage important after he finished his worship of Ramadan And would marry and also consummate the marriage in the month of shawwal

Abu Hurayrah (may Allaah be pleased with him), that the Prophet (peace and blessings of Allaah be upon him) said: "If there comes to you one whose religious commitment and character pleases you, then marry [your female relative who is under your care] to him, for if you do not do that, there will be tribulation on earth and much corruption."

Classed as hasan by al-Albaani in Saheeh al-Tirmidhi 1084.

Narrated Abu Huraira:

The Prophet (ﷺ) said, "A woman is married for four things, i.e., her wealth, her family status, her beauty and her religion. So you should marry the religious woman (otherwise) you will be a loser.

Having a wife make us responsible for not only ourselves but also for her, her children, her parents, the neighborhood she lives in, etc.

Allah said in Surah 4 An Nisa 34. **Men are in charge of women by [right of] what Allah has given one over the other and what they spend [for maintenance] from their wealth. So righteous women are devoutly obedient, guarding in [the husband's] absence what Allah would have them guard. But those [wives] from whom you fear arrogance - [first] advise them; [then if they persist], forsake them in bed; and [finally], strike them. But if they obey you [once more], seek no means against them. Indeed, Allah is ever Exalted and Grand.**

Allah also gave responsibility to the women as

Allah said in Surah 4 An Nisa 228. **And due to the wives is similar to what is expected of them, according to what is reasonable. But the men have a degree over them [in responsibility and authority]. And Allah is Exalted in Might and Wise.**

Abdullah ibn Umar reported: The Messenger of Allah, peace and blessings be upon him, said, "Every one of you is a shepherd and is responsible for his flock. The leader of people is a guardian and is responsible for his subjects. A man is the guardian of his family and he is responsible for them. A woman is the guardian of her husband's home and his children and she is responsible for them. The servant of a man is a guardian of the property of his master and he is responsible for it. No doubt, every one of you is a shepherd and is responsible for his flock."

Ṣaḥīḥ al-Bukhārī 6719, Ṣaḥīḥ Muslim 1829

Marriage is an act of worship and just like all acts of ibadah it's not made easy. Only on TV do you meet the girl of your dream and then happily after but the reality is that Marriage is like all the other acts of worship, it comes with challenges.

Narrated from Abu Hurayrah, according to which the Messenger of Allah (blessings and peace of Allah be upon him) said: "When Allah created Paradise and Hell, he sent Jibreel to Paradise and said, 'Look at it and at what I have prepared for its people therein.' So he went and looked at it and at what Allah had prepared for its people therein. Then he went back to Him and said, 'By Your Glory, no one will hear of it but he will enter it.' Then He commanded that it should be surrounded with difficult things. Then He said, 'Go back and look at what I have prepared for its people therein.' He went back and saw that it was surrounded with difficult things. He came back and said, 'By Your Glory, I am afraid that no one will enter it.'

Allah said, 'Go and look at Hell and see what I have prepared for its people therein.' [He saw it] with parts of it consuming other parts. He came back and said, 'By Your Glory, no one who hears of it will enter it.' So Allah commanded that it should be surrounded with desires. Then he said, 'Go back to it.' So he went back, then he said, 'By Your Glory, I am afraid that no one will be saved from it and that all will enter it.'"

Narrated by at-Tirmidhi (2736)

Despite the difficulty and challenges we have in marriage, if we look at it as an aspect of worship we will progress...as the people of the Dunya says...the family the prays together stays together.

In closing I have a few suggestions to help to maintain a healthy marriage 1st overlook the flaws of your spouse as long as they don't violate the Qur'an and sunnah

Anas said: "The Prophet was with one of the Mothers of the Believers when another one sent a wooden bowl in which was some food. She struck the hand of the Prophet and the bowl fell and broke. The Prophet picked up the two pieces and put them together, then he started to gather up the food and said: 'Your mother got jealous; eat.' So they ate. He waited until she brought the wooden bowl that was in her house, then he gave the sound bowl to the messenger and left the broken bowl in the house of the one who had broken it."

أَخْبَرَنَا مُحَمَّدُ بْنُ الْمُثَنَّى، قَالَ حَدَّثَنَا خَالِدٌ، قَالَ حَدَّثَنَا حُمَيْدٌ، قَالَ حَدَّثَنَا أَنَسٌ، قَالَ كَانَ النَّبِيُّ صلى الله عليه وسلم عِنْدَ إِحْدَى أُمَّهَاتِ الْمُؤْمِنِينَ فَأَرْسَلَتْ أُخْرَى بِقَصْعَةٍ فِيهَا طَعَامٌ فَضَرَبَتْ يَدَ الرَّسُولِ فَسَقَطَتِ الْقَصْعَةُ فَانْكَسَرَتْ فَأَخَذَ النَّبِيُّ صلى الله عليه وسلم الْكِسْرَتَيْنِ فَضَمَّ إِحْدَاهُمَا إِلَى الأُخْرَى فَجَعَلَ يَجْمَعُ فِيهَا الطَّعَامَ وَيَقُولُ " غَارَتْ أُمُّكُمْ كُلُوا " . فَأَكَلُوا فَأَمْسَكَ حَتَّى جَاءَتْ بِقَصْعَتِهَا الَّتِي فِي بَيْتِهَا فَدَفَعَ الْقَصْعَةَ الصَّحِيحَةَ إِلَى الرَّسُولِ وَتَرَكَ الْمَكْسُورَةَ فِي بَيْتِ الَّتِي كَسَرَتْهَا .

Sunan an-Nasa'i 3955

In-book reference: Book 36,# 17

English translation: Vol. 4, Book 36, #3407

Allah said in Surah 64 ayat 14. **O ye who believe! Truly, among your wives and your children are (some that are) enemies to yourselves: so beware of them! But if ye forgive and overlook, and cover up (their faults), verily Allah is Oft-Forgiving, Most Merciful.**

Allah said in Surah 4 An Nisa 19. **And live with them [wives] in kindness. For if you dislike them - perhaps you dislike a thing and Allah makes therein much good"**

2nd suggestion To facilitate a healthy marriage have fun with your wife, Play with her, Smile and laugh and make this deen a pleasure to her

Allah said in Surah 30 Rum 21. **And of His signs is that He created for you from yourselves mates that you may find tranquillity in them; and He placed between you affection and mercy. Indeed in that are signs for a people who give thought.**

Abu Daawood (2578) and Ahmad (26277) narrated that 'Aa'ishah said: I went out with the Prophet (blessings and peace of Allah be upon him) on one of his journeys when I was still young and had not put on weight. He said to the people: "Go on ahead." So they went on ahead, then he said to me, "Come, let me race with you." So I raced with him, and I beat him, and he said nothing. Then when I had put on some weight, and I had forgotten about it, I went out with him on one of his journeys, and he said to the people: "Go on ahead." So they went on ahead, then he said to me, "Come, let me race with you." So I raced with him, and he beat me, then he smiled and said: "This is in return for that."

Classed as saheeh by al-Albaani in Saheeh Abi Daawood.

3rd and final suggestion for a good healthy marriage is to communicate with each other and spend on here even if you feed her like feeding a queen.

The Prophet (peace and blessings of Allah be upon him) said: "You will never spend anything seeking thereby the Face of Allah, but you will be rewarded for it, even (the food) that you put in your wife's mouth." Narrated by al-Bukhari, 56.

Mu'awiyah ibn Haydah (may Allaah be pleased with him) said: I said, "O Messenger of Allah, what are the rights of the wife of any one of us over him?" He said: "That you should feed her when you feed yourself, clothe her when you clothe yourself, you should not hit her on the face, you should not curse her and you should not forsake her except in the house."

Ahmad (20025) and Abu Dawood (2142).

Muhammad The Last & Final Prophet

Allah said in Ali 'Imran 3:81

"And (remember) when Allah took the Covenant of the Prophets, saying:

'Take whatever I gave you from the Book and Hikmah (understanding of the Laws of Allah, etc.), and afterwards there will come to you a Messenger (Muhammad (blessings and peace of Allah be upon him)) confirming what is with you; you must, then, believe in him and help him.' Allah said: 'Do you agree (to it) and will you take up My Covenant (which I conclude with you)?' They said: 'We agree.' He said: "Then bear witness; and I am with you among the witnesses (for this)'"

Allah said in al-Maa'idah 5:82-85

"Verily, you will find the strongest among men in enmity to the believers (Muslims) the Jews and those who are Al-Mushrikoon, and you will find the nearest in love to the believers (Muslims) those who say: 'We are Christians.' That is because amongst them are priests and monks, and they are not proud.

And when they (who call themselves Christians) listen to what has been sent down to the Messenger (Muhammad (blessings and peace of Allah be upon him), you see their eyes overflowing with tears because of the truth they have recognised. They say: 'Our Lord! We believe; so write us down among the witnesses.

'And why should we not believe in Allah and in that which has come to us of the truth (Islamic Monotheism)? And we wish that our Lord will admit us (in Paradise on the Day of Resurrection) along with the righteous people (Prophet Muhammad (blessings and peace of Allah be upon him) and his Companions).'

So because of what they said, Allah rewarded them Gardens under which rivers flow (in Paradise), they will abide therein forever. Such is the reward of good doers"

It was narrated that Abu Moosa (may Allah be pleased with him) said: The Messenger of Allah (blessings and peace of Allah be upon him) instructed us to set out for the land of Abyssinia. News of that reached Quraysh, so they sent word to 'Amr ibn al-'Aas and 'Umaarah ibn al-Waleed, who collected gifts for the Negus. We and they came to the Negus, and they brought a gift, which he accepted, and they prostrated to him. Then 'Amr ibn al-'Aas said: Some of our people have turned away from our religion, and they are in your land. The Negus said to them: In my land? He said: Yes. So he sent for us, and Ja'far said to us: No one of you should speak; I will be your spokesman today. We came to the Negus when he was sitting in his court, with 'Amr ibn al-'Aas on his right and 'Umaarah on his left, and the priests and monks were sitting in two rows. 'Amr and 'Umaarah said to him: They will not prostrate to you. When we came to him, the priests and monks who were with him said: Prostrate to the king. Ja'far said: We only prostrate to Allah. The Negus said to him: Why is that? He said: Allah has sent to us His Messenger; he is the Messenger who was foretold by 'Eesaa (Jesus), who said that a Messenger would come after him whose name would be Ahmad. He instructed us to worship Allah and not associate anything with Him, and to establish prayer and give zakaah. And he instructed us to do what is right and forbade us to do what is wrong. The people were impressed by his words, and when 'Amr saw that, he said: May Allah bless the king; they disagree with you concerning 'Eesa ibn Maryam (Jesus son of Mary). The Negus said to Ja'far: What does your companion say about the son of Maryam? He said: He says concerning him what Allah says: He is a soul created by Allah and His word whom he brought forth from the Virgin whom no man had touched. The Negus picked up a stick from the ground and held it up, then he said: O priests and monks, what these people say about the son of Maryam does not differ from what you say by as much as the weight of this stick. Welcome to you and the one from whom you have come. I bear witness that he is the Messenger of Allah and that he is the one who was foretold by 'Eesaa ibn Maryam. Were it not for my position of kingship, I would go to him and carry his sandals. Stay in my land for as long as you want. And he ordered that they be given food and clothing, and he said: Return their gift to these people (Quraysh).

Narrated by al-Haakim in al-Mustadrak (3208)

Allah said in al-Qasas 28:52-55

"Those to whom We gave the Scripture (i.e. the Taurat (Torah) and the Injeel (Gospel), etc.) before it, - they believe in it (the Quran).

And when it is recited to them, they say: 'We believe in it. Verily, it is the truth from our Lord. Indeed even before it we have been from those who submit themselves to Allah in Islam as Muslims' (like Abdullah bin Salam and Salman Al-Farisee, etc.). These will be given their reward twice over, because they are patient, and repel evil with good, and spend (in charity) out of what We have provided them. And when they hear AlLaghw (dirty, false, evil vain talk), they withdraw from it and say: 'To us our deeds, and to you your deeds. Peace be to you. We seek not the ignorant'"

It was narrated from Abu Moosa al-Ash'ari (may Allah be pleased with him) that the Messenger of Allah (blessings and peace of Allah be upon him) said: "There are three who will be given a double reward: a man from among the people of the Book who believed in his Prophet, then lived to see the Prophet (blessings and peace of Allah be upon him) and followed him and believed in him– he will have a double reward; and a slave who fulfils his duty towards Allah and towards his master – he will have a double reward; and a man who had a slave woman whom he fed and fed her well, and taught her and taught her well, then he set her free and married her – he will have a double reward.".

Narrated by al-Bukhaari (3011) and Muslim (154)

Allah said in an-Nisa' 4:170-175

"O mankind! Verily, there has come to you the Messenger (Muhammad (blessings and peace of Allah be upon him)) with the truth from your Lord, so believe in him, it is better for you. But if you disbelieve, then certainly to Allah belongs all that is in the heavens and the earth. And Allah is Ever All-Knowing, All- Wise.

O people of the Scripture (Jews and Christians)! Do not exceed the limits in your religion, nor say of Allah aught but the truth. The Messiah 'Eesa (Jesus), son of Maryam (Mary), was (no more than) a Messenger of Allah and His Word, ('Be!' - and he was) which He bestowed on Maryam (Mary) and a spirit (Rooh) created by Him; so believe in Allah and His Messengers. Say not: 'Three (trinity)!' Cease! (it is) better for you. For Allah is (the only) One Ilah (God), Glory be to Him (Far Exalted is He) above having a son. To Him belongs all that is in the heavens and all that is in the earth. And Allah is All-Sufficient as a Disposer of affairs.

The Messiah will never be proud to reject to be a slave to Allah, nor the angels who are near (to Allah). And whosoever rejects His worship and is proud, then He will gather them all together unto Himself.

So, as for those who believed (in the Oneness of Allah - Islamic Monotheism) and did deeds of righteousness, He will give their (due) rewards, and more out of His Bounty. But as for those who refuse His worship and were proud, He will punish them with a painful torment. And they will not find for themselves besides Allah any protector or helper.

O mankind! Verily, there has come to you a convincing proof (Prophet Muhammad (blessings and peace of Allah be upon him)) from your Lord, and We sent down to you a manifest light (this Quran).

So, as for those who believed in Allah and held fast to Him, He will admit them to His Mercy and Grace (i.e. Paradise), and guide them to Himself by a Straight Path"

Glossary

1. Alhamdulillah ٱلْـحَـمْـدُ لله is an Arabic phrase meaning "Praise be to God" OR "Thank God". Alhamdulillah is commonly used term by Muslims around the world including Arab Christians, and other non-Muslim speakers of the Arabic language.

Al-, means "the"

Hamdu meaning "praise & commendation" li-llāh(i) means "Allah" (SWT).

2. Allah- The word *Allah*, according to several Arabic lexicons, means "the Being Who comprises all the attributes of perfection", i.e. the Being Who is perfect in every way (in His knowledge, power etc.), and possesses the best and the noblest qualities imaginable in the highest degree. This meaning is supported by the Holy Quran when it says:

"His are the best (or most beautiful) names." (17:110; 20:8; and 7:180)

Contrary to popular belief, the word *Allah* is NOT a contraction of *al-ilah* (al meaning 'the', and *ilah* meaning 'god').

Had it been so, then the expression *ya Allah* ('O Allah!') would have been ungrammatical, because according to the Arabic language when you address someone by the vocative form *ya* followed by a title, the *al* ('the') must be dropped from the title. For example, you cannot say *ya ar-rabb* but must say *ya rabb* (for 'O Lord'). So if the word *Allah* was *al-ilah* ('the God'), we would not be able to say: *ya Allah*, which we do.

Lane's Arabic-English Lexicon (which is based on classical Arabic dictionaries), says under the word *Allah*, while citing many linguistical authorities:

"Allah ... is a proper name applied to *the Being Who exists necessarily, by Himself, comprising all the attributes of perfection*, a proper name denoting *the true god* ... the *al* being inseparable from it, not derived..."

Allah is thus a proper name, not derived from anything, and the *Al* is inseparable from it. The word *al-ilah* (the god) is a different word.

The word *Allah* is unique among the names of God in all the languages of mankind, in that it was never applied to any being other than God. The pre-Islamic Arabs used it to refer to the Supreme Being, and never applied it to any of the other things they worshipped. Other names of God used by mankind, such as "lord", "god", "khuda", etc. have all also been used for beings other than God. They have meanings which refer to some particular attribute of God, but "Allah" is the name which refers to the Being Himself as His personal name.

The Holy Quran itself refers to the uniqueness of the name *Allah* when it says: "**Do you know anyone who can be named along with Him?**" (19:65)

Arabic is the only language, and Islam is the only religion, that has given the personal name of God (as distinct from attributive names such as lord, god, the most high, etc.)

There are clear prophecies in previous scriptures (the Bible, the Vedas etc.) about the man who will come and give the name of God, which in previous religions was regarded as a secret.

1. David prophesied:

   "Blessed is he who comes in the *name* of the Lord" (Psalms 118:26).

   This is also repeated in the Gospels (Matt. 21:9, etc.), and was fulfilled by the Holy Prophet Muhammad whose first revelation was "Read in the name of thy Lord" (the Quran, 96:1).

2. Zechariah prophesied:

   "And the Lord shall be king over all the earth, in that day there shall be one Lord, and *his name one*." (Zech. 14:9)

   All Muslims, anywhere on the earth, speaking totally different languages, recognise the name "Allah", thus fulfilling this prophecy, "his name one". (All Christians, to take an example, do not recognise a single name of God, and therefore do not fulfil this prophecy.)

3. Isaiah prophesied:

   "And in that day shall you say, Praise the Lord, call upon His *name*." (Isaiah 12:4) So Muslims say repeatedly exactly this: *al-hamdu li-llah*, and call upon His name Allah.

3. *RadyiAllahu Anhu or RA* رضى الله عنه is well known as an Arabic phrase meaning, "May God Allah Be Pleased With Him." This phrase is usually uttered after a companion's name there are grammatical variations used after the names of female companions or when more than one person is mentioned at the same time.

   The term 'Radhi Allah Anhu' has three main forms

Radhi Allah AnHU (to a male) Radhi Allah AnHA
(to a female)

OR more than one person, it is Radhiallahu
'anhum. رَّضِيَ اللَّهُ عَنْهُم

Radhi Allah AnHUM (To them) The only term used
in the Quran.

Phrase Radhi Allah Anhu has two meanings One in the mode of giving
news and the other in the form of supplication translation of using this
phrase in the first form would be (Allah is pleased with him/her) and in
the second (may Allah be pleased with him/her)

1. May Allah be pleased with him/her/them (When used in
   prayer). This is used in common Arabic
2. Allah is pleased with him/her/them (when used in news) - This
   form is found in the Quran.

When this phrase is used for the blessed RIGHTEOUS Companions
(Allah be well pleased with them) it can be used in both forms. As such,
one may say regarding a Companion, Allah is pleased with him/her or
may Allah be pleased with him/her

**Allah was well pleased with the believers when they swore allegiance
unto thee beneath the tree, and He knew what was in their hearts,
and He sent down peace of reassurance on them, and hath rewarded
them with a near victory 48:18**

**O Prophet! If believing women come unto thee, taking oath of
allegiance unto thee that they will ascribe no thing as partner unto**

Allah, and will neither steal nor commit adultery nor kill their children, nor produce any lie that they have devised between their hands and feet, nor disobey thee in what is right, then accept their allegiance and ask Allah to forgive them. Lo! Allah is Forgiving, Merciful 60:12

Other references are also present in 9:100 such as those who left their homes for the sake of Allah and of those that aided them (Muhajirs and Ansars) with whom ALLAH is pleased with.

And the first to lead the way, of the Muhajirin and the Ansar, and those who followed them in goodness - Allah is well pleased with them and they are well pleased with Him, and He hath made ready for them Gardens underneath which rivers flow, wherein they will abide forever. That is the supreme triumph.9:100

radiya Allahu AAanhum (R.A) رَّضِيَ اللَّهُ عَنْهُم As News for believers

Their reward is with their Lord: Gardens of Eden underneath which rivers flow, wherein they dwell for ever. Allah hath pleasure in them and they have pleasure in Him.(Allah is well pleased with them and they are well pleased with Him) This is (in store) for him who feareth his Lord.

Surat Al-Bayyinah (The Clear Proof) -98:8

Thou wilt not find folk who believe in Allah and the Last Day loving those who oppose Allah and His messenger, even though they be their fathers or their sons or their brethren or their clan. As for such, He hath written faith upon their hearts and hath strengthened them with a Spirit from Him, and He will bring them into Gardens underneath which rivers flow, wherein they will abide. Allah is well pleased with them, and they are well pleased with Him. They are Allah's party. Lo! is it not Allah's party who are the successful? Surat Al-Mujādila (The Pleading Woman) 58:22

This is a day in which their truthfulness profiteth the truthful, for theirs are Gardens underneath which rivers flow, wherein they are secure for ever, Allah taking pleasure in them and they in Him. That is the great triumph. Surat Al-Mā'idah (The Table Spread) 5:119

4. .SAW -Peace be upon him (Arabic: صلى الله عليه وسلم salla Allahu alayhi wa sallam, also transliterated as sallalahu aleyhi wasallam or salallahu alayhi wasalaam) is a phrase that Muslims often say after saying the name of a prophet of Islam.

An alternative translation is "May God bless him and grant him peace." In Arabic these salutations are called salawat. 'Peace be upon him' is abbreviated to "saw" or "pbuh."

"Allah sends His Salât (Graces, Honours, Blessings, Mercy) on the Prophet (Muhammad (blessings and peace of Allah be upon him)) and also His angels (ask Allah to bless and forgive him). O you who believe! Send your Salât on (ask Allah to bless) him (Muhammad (blessings and peace of Allah be upon him)), and (you should) greet (salute) him with the Islamic way of greeting (salutation i.e. As¬Salâmu 'Alaikum)" al-Ahzaab 33:56

He (blessings and peace of Allah be upon him) said: "Whoever sends blessings upon me once, Allah will send blessings upon him tenfold and will erase from him ten misdeeds and raise him ten degrees in status." Narrated by an-Nasaa'i (1297); classed as saheeh by al-Albaani in Saheeh Sunan an-Nasaa'i.

Narrated that Ubayy ibn Ka'b (may Allah be pleased with him) said: I said: O Messenger of Allah, I want to send more blessings upon you (before offering supplication); how much of my supplication should I allocate to that? He said: "Whatever you wish." I said: One quarter? He said, "Whatever you wish, but if you do more, it will be better for you." I said: Half? He said: "Whatever you wish but if you do more, it will be better for you." I said: Two thirds? He said: "Whatever you wish, but if you do more, it will be better for you." I said: Shall I make all of my supplication for that? He said: Then your worries will be taken care of and your sin will be forgiven." At-Tirmidhi (2457)

Classed as hasan by al-Albaani in Sunan at-Tirmidhi. Allah, may He be exalted, says:

"O you who believe! Send your Salât on (ask Allah to bless) him (Muhammad (blessings and peace of Allah be upon him)), and (you should) greet (salute) him with the Islamic way of greeting (salutation i.e. As¬Salâmu 'Alaikum)" al-Ahzaab 33:56.

5. Tahajjad-Tahajjud means specifically praying at night, and some scholars limited it to prayers that are offered at night after sleeping.

Al-Isra 17:79 **And during a part of the night, keep awake by the prayer. It is beyond what is incumbent on you; maybe your** <u>Lord</u> **will raise you to a position of great glory.**

<u>Al-Furqan</u> 25:64 **And they who pass the night prostrating themselves before their Lord and standing**

Tahajjud may be performed in the early part of the night, the middle part of the night, or the later part of the night, but after the obligatory 'Isha' Prayer (night Prayer).

Ibn Hajar says: There was no specific time in which the Prophet (peace and blessings be upon him) would perform his late night Prayer; but he used to do whatever was easiest for him.

'Amr ibn 'Absah claimed that he heard Muhammad as saying: The closest that a servant comes to his Lord is during the middle of the latter portion of the night. If you can be among those who remember Allah the Exalted One at that time, then do so

At-Tirmidhi

Tahajjud Prayer does not entail a specific number of rak'ahs that must be performed, nor is there any maximum limit that may be performed. It would be fulfilled even if one prayed just one rak'ah of Witr after 'Isha'; however, it is traditionally prayed with at least two rak'at which is known as shif'a followed by witr as this is what Muhammad did.

Abdullah ibn Umar narrated that Muhammad said: "Salatul Layl (Night Prayer, i.e. Tahajjud) is offered as two rak'at followed by two rak'at and (so on) and if anyone is afraid of the approaching dawn (Fajr prayer) he should pray one rak'at and this will be a Witr for all the rak'at which he has prayed before."

Bukhari, hadith 990

Al-Hajjaaj ibn 'Amr al-Ansaari (may Allah be pleased with him) said: One of you thinks that if he gets up at night and prays until morning comes that he has done tahajjud. But in fact tahajjud means praying after sleeping, then praying after sleeping. That is how the Messenger of Allah (blessings and peace of Allah upon him) prayed. Al-Haafiz Ibn Hajar said in al-Talkhees al-Habeer (2/35): Its isnaad is hasan; it includes Abu Saalih, the scribe of al-Layth, and it is somewhat weak. It was also narrated by al-Tabaraani, whose isnaad includes Ibn Luhay'ah, whose report is supported by the one that came before it. End quote.

It has been reported on the Authority of Abu Hurayra (RA) that the Apostle of Allah (may peace and blessing be upon him) said: Whoever seeks Forgiveness before the rising of the sun from the west, God will turn to him with mercy.

Sahih Muslim p.347,#1

About the Author

Who are you and What qualifies you to speak on this topic?

Alhumdulillah All praise and thanks belong to Allah. I was born on September 5, 1975 in Long Island New York to Lut and Hagar Nero. My Father is from Antiguan descent, Born and raised in New York City and studied to be a Catholic Priest but somehow found his way in the Air Force instead. He returned home from active duty in the 60's when Malcom X and Martin Luther King were calling for justice for Afro-Americans, and the Black Panthers were in mid swing of the Movement. My Father was affected by the social environment and choose the Dar-al Islam as a umbrella after taking his Shahada. The Dar (as he calls it) was a sect of Al Islam who utilized the Qur'an and Hadith as a way of life. They Studies the teaching of Imaam Muhammad ibn Abd al-Wahhab and believed in separation from the people of the disbelief (as much as possible). The Dar brought Muslims together to live in communities, buy food and clothing together, worship together, encouraged Marriage, encouraged sobriety, gave birth and buried their dead separate from the people of disbelieve and even established laws and consequence according to the Shariah law. The community of Dar al- Islam introduced my Father to my Mother, who had studied Islam from the perspective of the Five Percenters (Nation of Gods and Earths) until she too took her Shahada. I was born in Long Island New York but moved to Landover Maryland in1977. I was homeschooled for the first couple years and then started at ISA (Islamic Saudi Academy) in the 4th grade. My Parents started an organization called NIYA National Islamic Youth Alliance, which catered to building the Muslim Youth up and teaching them how to live by the Qur'an and Sunnah. After College I was asked to take the position of Imaam at several Institutes and after bouncing around for the first two and a half years until I found a home at Masjid Ar-Rahman.

In my pursuit of knowledge I've noticed a deficiency in the Dawah being propagated here in the west. **African American** (Black) muslims were speaking ill of one another primarily because of the scholars they learned from. The **bidah** (hatred) of the scholars from Pakistan, Egypt, Africa, Saudi Arabia, etc was being passed down to the African **American** (Black) Muslims who didn't know the difference between Culture and Deen. These homegrown converts, the **African American** (Black) who had very little knowledge but would be speaking against each other based on Menhaj (the way or the path) instead of Elm(Knowledge) and this became a regular practice. I attributed this behavior as a result of the effects from Slavery. Black Muslims felt as if their Islam was insignificant and the Islam of the Immigrant Muslims was superior however Allah and his Messenger spoke against this sort of mentality in Surah 9 At-Taubah 97. **The Arabs (Bedouins) are the worst in disbelief and hypocrisy, and more likely to be in ignorance or the limits (Allah's Commandments and His Legal Laws) which Allah has revealed to His Messenger. And Allah is All-Knower, All- Wise.**

Islamic tradition known as Hadith states that in his final sermon the Prophet Muhammad, Allah's Blessings and Peace be upon him, said:

"There is no superiority for an Arab over a non-Arab, nor for a non-Arab over an Arab. Neither is the white superior over the black, nor is the black superior over the white -- except by piety."

To be fair the main superiority the Arabs had over the world of believers is as Allah said in Surah 26 Ash-Shu'ara 192 **And truly, this (the Qur'an) is a revelation from the Lord of the Alamin (mankind, Jinn and all that exists), 193. which the trustworthy Ruh [Jabreal (Gabriel)] has brought down 194. Upon your heart {O Muhammad (peace and blessings of Allaah be upon him)} that you may be (one) of the warners, 195. In the plain Arabic language.**

The Immigrant Muslims who were teaching the Black Muslims, were steeped in the bid'ah and were transferring their Culture and hatred to a people who thought they were getting Deen (The religion). The Islam from the Immigrant muslims was rich in cultural practices, so much so that they literally didn't know what was Islam and what practices they learned from generations of innovations. However a time came which was parallel to the time when Islam was brought to Mecca here in the west. The crimes in the west are similar to the crimes practiced in Mecca when Rasullullah came with this Islamic Monotheism and the Time the Qur'an was revealed to Rasullullah (SAW). In Mecca, like in the West tribalism ruled and those Tribe with Political power reign supreme dominated. Alcoholism was the culture in Mecca just like Drinking and Drugging was the norm here in the West. The Meccan would drink Alcohol because if you drink the water you could get sick from its contaminants. The Prophet and his companions used to eat Dates and water as his wife said,

Narrated 'Aisha:

The Prophet died when we had satisfied our hunger with the two black things, i.e. dates and water.

Muslim in Mecca had to choose just as the Muslims of the West had to make the choice to stay away from Drugs and Alcohol, and strive to eat Halal. Similarly Muslims in Mecca had to choose to dress modestly until the verse came down

Allah said in Surah 24:31 **And tell the believing women to reduce [some] of their vision and guard their private parts and not expose their adornment except that which [necessarily] appears thereof and to wrap [a portion of] their head covers over their chests and not expose their adornment except to their husbands, their fathers, their husbands' fathers, their sons, their husbands' sons, their brothers, their brothers' sons, their sisters' sons, their women, that which their right hands possess, or those male attendants having no physical desire, or children who are not yet aware of the private aspects of women. And let them not stamp their feet to make known what they conceal of their adornment. And turn to Allah in repentance, all of you, O believers, that you might succeed.**

In Mecca, at the time The Messenger of Allah (Peace and Blessing be upon him) was calling to Tauhid the Meccan Pagans would make Tawaf around the Kabah Naked.

Narrated Abu Huraira: "On the Day of Nahr (10th of Dhul-Hijja, in the year prior to the last Hajj of the Prophet when Abu Bakr was the leader of the pilgrims in that Hajj) Abu Bakr sent me along with other announcers to Mina to make a public announcement: "No pagan is allowed to perform Hajj after this year and no naked person is allowed to perform the Tawaf (going around) around the Kaaba (the black cube building in Mecca). Then Allah's Apostle sent 'All to read out the Surat Bara'a (At-Tauba) to the people; so he made the announcement along with us on the day of Nahr in Mina: "No pagan is allowed to perform Hajj after this year and no naked person is allowed to perform the Tawaf around the Kaaba." (Translation of Sahih Bukhari, Volume 1, Book 8, Number 365)"

In the West Muslims dress in the Jilbab, Hijab, Niqab, Qamis, Thobe, Isar, Ridaa as a choice and an act of worship in contrast to being the law in the Muslim Lands where is was madated by law.

Marriage was encouraged in Mecca just as muslims here in the west are expected to protect themselves from being openly lewd and restrict themselves from illegal sexual intercourse by getting married. As the West moves further away from righteousness by openly welcoming Gay Marriage, leagaling alcoholism and drug usage, restricting polygamy, encouraging women to wear less and less clothing, it has become strange to worship Allah in your word and deed.

Abu Huraira reported: The Messenger of Allah, peace and blessings be upon him, said, "Islam began as a something strange and it will return to being strange, so blessed are the strangers."

Source: Ṣaḥīḥ Muslim 145

As the West continued to wage war against Islam, the media portrays Muslims as Terrorist both in Movies and the world news. American (Black) Muslims are subject to all of these ills but somehow we still chose Allah and his messenger. Before September 11 and the inauguration of President Donald Trump, we{Black Muslims} were overlooked and thought to be fake muslims, meaning not as righteous as our immigrant brothers. However, Immigrant Muslims in the West went through much oppression after 911 and were even restricted from coming into America after Donald Trump became a President. Many muslim Immigrants took off their Islamic Garb, changed their name, and welcomed the Islamic practice of Black Muslim who have dealt with the oppression from this oppressive society. Black Imams began to join the call to Tauhid and it seemed their knowledge was not only accepted but also thriving. Islam in the West was growing and places like Egypt, Pakistan, Saudi Arabia were drowning in their cultural ills and even worse Bid'a (Innovation). For example there was a world wide Qur'an competition in Dubai in 2018 and the 1st place winner was a young man from Minneapolis MN

USA, 2nd place was a tie with a young man from Libya and a young man from Tunisia. It was no longer necessary to leave America to grow your Islam because many of the Hafiz (Guardian or memorizer) of Qur'an live here in the west and Teach in Madrasa (Schools) here.

Now there is no way to compare ourselves with the first three generation or how they strived in the Way of Allah but there was growth happening here in the West.

Abdullah ibn Mas'ud reported: The Prophet, (peace and blessings be upon him), said, "The best people are those of my generation, then those who come after them, then those who come after them. Then, there will come people after them whose testimony precedes their oaths and their oaths precede their testimony."

Source: Ṣaḥīḥ al-Bukhārī 6065, Ṣaḥīḥ Muslim 2533

As it mentioned in al-Saheehayn, the Prophet (peace and blessings of Allaah be upon him) said: "Do not curse the Sahaabah, for by the One in Whose hand is my soul, if any one of you spent the equivalent of Mount Uhud in gold, he would not attain the level of any one of them, or even come half way."

Majmoo' al-Fataawa, 13/65, 66

Islam is not Stationary and does not belong to a particular group of people or particular time frame. As we see when Allah, Highly Exalted above what they claim about him, sent the first Ayats of Surah 96 Iqra in The Cave of Lights in Mecca. The Meccan Pagan rejected the Dawah and actually started to oppress the few Muslims that were present and didn't have the Visa. They were so harsh against the pioneers of this deen that The Messenger of Allah sent a group of Muslims to Abyssinia for asylum. Once the Ummah got larger in number and Stronger they moved to Medina. After that Allah sent The Muslim troops to {Room,} Persia, Southeast Asia and all across the world. Muslims are projected to be the world's fastest-growing major religious group in the decades ahead, as Pew Research Center has explained, and signs of this rapid growth already are visible. In the period between 2010 and 2015, births to Muslims made up an estimated 31% of all babies born around the world – far exceeding the Muslim share of people of all ages in 2015 (24%). So Islam has been brought all around the world so much so that we reach over 2 billion in number but it is my claim the Muslims in the West now leads the Charge.